Loss, Grief and Beyond

(The 7th Stage of Grief)

Robin Chodak

ISBN: 978-0-9987088-5-0

Library of Congress Control Number: 2026903510

Published in the United States of America
Website: www.robinchodak.com

Also by Robin Chodak

Be Gentle with Me, I'm, Grieving

Moving to Excellence,
A Pathway to Transformation after Grief

3 Must Have Connections for Inner Peace

Ten Grief Lessons from Golf

Table of Contents

Dedication

I dedicate this book to my deceased loved ones. They have shaped my existence: my sister, Ralene; my husband, Steve; and my husband, Gerry. Those are the three significant losses that I have encountered in my physical realm.

I have accepted that traumatic grief has been part of my journey in life and understand that my purpose is to help others with their grief experiences. I am grateful for the short time that I have had with my sister and two husbands. They enriched my life, and I view the world differently. They are always available when I need them in the spirit world, and we share an eternal bond.

Introduction

I did not expect to write another book so soon after publishing Ten Grief Lessons from Golf in 2022. But I have learned to listen to Spirit—that still, quiet voice that speaks from somewhere deeper than thought. It urged me to write this book, and I have learned not to argue with it.

The reason it called me is simple: too many people are grieving alone, without a framework for what they are experiencing. They have lost someone they love—a spouse, a sibling, a child, a parent—and the world has handed them a timeline and a set of stages, expecting them to move through it neatly. But something in them resists. Something keeps reaching back toward the person they lost, searching for continued connection, wondering if what they feel is real or simply wishful thinking. It is real. This book is my attempt to show you why.

Spirit is the divine essence that resides within you and continues to exist even after death. Throughout this book, I use the terms Spirit, God, Higher Power, and the Universe interchangeably—not because I believe they are identical, but because I believe they point toward the same truth. I want every reader to find themselves reflected in at least one of those words. And if none of them feel comfortable to you yet, that is okay. Stay with me.

You do not need to arrive at this book already believing in an afterlife, in signs from the deceased, or in the idea that love survives death. Many people who find comfort in these pages begin as skeptics. What you do need is a willingness to remain open—to consider that what you have experienced in your quietest, most private moments of grief may be pointing toward something real and worthy of your attention.

Grief touches nearly every life, whether it comes suddenly or after many years. It is not something to be feared, rushed, or resolved on someone else's schedule. It is a natural and profound part of being human, and within it are the seeds of transformation—if you are willing to look.

This book will take you on a journey. We will begin by understanding grief itself—what it is and how it affects your mind and body. From there, we will explore death—not with dread, but with curiosity and even a sense of wonder. We will move through pain and suffering, signs and intuition, and the delicate balance between science and mystery. And ultimately, we will arrive at what I call the

7th stage of grief—a way of living that I have named, practiced, and taught, and that has profoundly changed my life and the lives of those I have worked with.

The stories in this book are true. The losses are real. The signs are real. And the hope I offer is not the fragile kind that asks you to pretend everything is okay. It is a grounded, resilient hope—one forged in real darkness and carried into the light. It is the only kind of hope I believe is worth sharing.

If this book has found its way to you, I believe there is a reason. And by the time you reach the final page, I hope you will feel that too.

How to Use This Book

This is not a book meant to be read once and set aside. It is a book meant to be lived in.

Grief is not linear, and neither is this book. You may find that certain chapters speak to you immediately, while others take time before they resonate. That is not only normal—it is expected. Where you are in your grief journey will shape what you are ready to receive. I encourage you to return to chapters that call you back.

Often, the same words will meet you differently the second or third time you read them.

Before you begin, I recommend keeping a journal nearby. Throughout this book, I will ask you questions and invite you to reflect. These are not rhetorical—they are invitations. Writing your answers allows you to see your thoughts more clearly and creates a record of your growth that you can revisit over time. If you do not have a journal, a simple notebook is enough. The act of writing itself is part of the healing.

As you move through these pages, a few gentle suggestions: Take your time with the reflection questions rather than moving quickly past them. They are placed intentionally—these are the moments where the work moves from your mind into your heart.

If a chapter feels too heavy, set it down and return to it later. There is no value in forcing yourself through pain before you are ready. Grief has its own rhythm, and honoring that rhythm is part of your healing.

If a chapter feels easy or even comforting, pay attention to that as well. Sometimes what feels light is where something deeper is waiting to be discovered.

Share what moves you. Whether with a trusted friend, a support group, or someone who understands grief, speaking your experience aloud can be incredibly powerful. Grief carried alone often feels heavier than it needs to be. And most importantly, be gentle with yourself. You are here because you have loved someone deeply—and lost them. That is one of the most profound human experiences there is. You deserve patience, compassion, and care as you move through it. When you are ready, turn the page.
Your journey into the *7th stage of grief* begins.

Chapter 1: Not Knowing

"By replacing fear of the unknown with curiosity we open ourselves up to an infinite stream of possibility. We can let fear rule our lives or we can become childlike with curiosity, pushing our boundaries, leaping out of our comfort zones, and accepting what life puts before us." ~ Alan Watts

Have you ever heard the saying, "What you don't know can't hurt you?" I've never believed that. In fact, some of the things I didn't know ended up changing my life forever. There were moments—many of them—when I wished I had known what was coming. Moments when I thought maybe, just maybe, I could have stopped it, prevented it, saved someone I loved. For a long time, my mind lived there, trapped in the *what-ifs*. But life doesn't work that way. It unfolds whether you are ready or not, whether you understand it or not, and whether you accept it or not.

Pause for a moment and think about your own life. Has there ever been a time when everything felt normal—predictable, even—and then, in an instant, everything changed? A phone call, a diagnosis, a loss you never saw coming. None of us are ever truly prepared for those moments. We live as if we know what tomorrow will bring, but the truth is, we don't. And it is in that not knowing where both our greatest fear and our greatest transformation exist.

In 1995, I met a man on a golf course. He was handsome, charismatic, and full of life. I had no idea in that moment that meeting him would begin a journey that would take me through the deepest love I had ever known—and the deepest grief I would ever experience. His name was Steve, my second husband. At the time, I wasn't thinking about loss or grief. I was thinking about possibility, about happiness, about finally getting something right in my life. But life, as I would come to learn, holds both joy and devastation in the same hands.

People often ask me now how I survived what I went through, how I'm not bitter, how I am able to live a happy life after so much loss. The answer didn't come to me right away. In fact, there was a time when I didn't think I would survive at all. There were moments when simply getting through the day felt impossible, when breathing felt heavy, when existing felt like too much.

The moment everything began to change for me didn't happen in a therapist's office or in a book. It happened on a beach. I remember standing there, my feet sinking slowly into the sand, the ocean stretching endlessly in front of me. The air felt heavy, like it was pressing against my body. My mind was louder than it had ever been—thoughts racing, colliding, spiraling out of control. I couldn't escape them. Grief had taken over everything.

The voices in my head were relentless—fear, guilt, confusion, pain—all speaking at once, all demanding my attention. I felt like I was losing myself, like I was coming undone from the inside out. I didn't recognize who I was anymore. The life I had known was gone, and I had no idea how to exist in the one that remained.

In that moment, I did the only thing I knew how to do. I asked for help. Not in a polished, graceful way. Not in a prayer I had memorized, but in desperation. I remember saying, "Please…God… take these thoughts away. I can't live like this anymore. Clear my mind. Replace them with something else… anything else." And then something happened that I still struggle to fully explain.

It was as if my mind stopped. Not slowed down, not softened—stopped. The noise disappeared completely. It felt like my brain had crashed, like someone had pulled the plug on every thought I had been carrying. There was nothing there—no fear, no pain, no story. Just emptiness.

At first, it scared me. But then something shifted. The fear began to dissolve, and in its place came something I had not felt in a very long time: peace. Not the kind of peace that depends on circumstances being okay, but a deeper peace, a quiet I could feel in my body. The sun warmed my skin. The clouds seemed to part just enough to let light through. I stood there grounded, present, aware in a way I had never been before. It felt like a reset, like something inside me had been cleared out to make room for something new.

That moment marked the beginning of my transformation. Not the end of my grief, but the beginning of a different relationship with it.
Years later, I would come to understand the words often attributed to the Dalai Lama: pain is inevitable, suffering is optional. But I had to live through the darkest moment of my life before those words meant anything real. That moment came the day I found Steve.

There are some experiences that don't feel like memories. They feel like something your body never forgets. That day is one of them. I found my husband dead in our basement from gunshot wounds to his head. Even writing those words now, I can feel the echo of that moment in my body.

Shock didn't just touch me—it consumed me. Time stopped making sense. My mind couldn't process what my eyes were seeing. It was as if reality had split open, and I had fallen into something I couldn't escape. There are no words strong enough to describe that kind of pain. It is not just emotional. It is physical. It lives in your chest, your stomach, your breath. It takes over your entire being.
In that moment, pain was inevitable. But what I didn't know then was that suffering would become a choice I would eventually have to face.

In the months and years that followed, I did everything I could to survive. I sought help. I worked with therapists, clergy, support groups, and coaches. I was searching for something—anything—that would make the pain stop or at least make it bearable. What I didn't realize at the time was that I wasn't just trying to heal. I was being reshaped. But my story with grief didn't begin there. It had been quietly weaving itself through my life long before Steve's death.

As a child, I experienced my first loss in a different way. My father was not a consistent presence in our home. He would leave for days, weeks, sometimes months, and then return. That pattern became part of our normal until one day he left and never came back. That was my first experience with loss—not death, but absence. And absence can be just as powerful.

My mother was left to raise four children on her own, working nights as a waitress just to keep us afloat. At twelve years old, I stepped into a role I was never meant to fill. I became the caretaker. I cooked, I cleaned, I watched over my siblings. I grew up quickly, but at a cost. I missed the parts of childhood that allow you to feel free—the after-school activities, the laughter with friends, the sense of lightness that should come with being young. That was another kind of grief: the loss of what could have been.

At fifteen, I met John. With him, my world expanded. For the first time, I felt seen, loved, and safe. He became my escape from the life I didn't want to be in. A year later, I was pregnant. At sixteen, my life changed overnight. I became a wife, a mother, an adult—whether I was ready or not. Looking back, I can see how much I was searching for love, for stability, for something to replace what I had lost.

And in many ways, I found it. I have a beautiful daughter and granddaughter because of that chapter of my life. But even then, loss was still present, quietly shaping me in the background.

At twenty-four, grief returned in a way I could not ignore. My sister, Ralene, was diagnosed with osteosarcoma—bone cancer. She was young, vibrant, full of life. Over the next four years, I watched that life slowly slip away. I watched my mother's heartbreak. I witnessed pain at a level I had never seen before. And I felt a growing anger inside me—anger at life, at circumstances, at the unfairness of it all.

When Ralene died at twenty, another part of me changed. Grief was no longer an occasional visitor. It had become a constant presence. Looking back now, I can see something I couldn't see then. Grief was not random in my life. It was shaping me, preparing me, opening me in ways I didn't yet understand.

When Steve died, I thought that was it—that I had reached the limit of what one person could endure. But grief had one more transformation waiting for me. And what I discovered on the other side of it would change everything. Living with grief has a way of breaking you open. It strips away what is not real. It forces you to question everything—your beliefs, your identity, your understanding of life and death. But if you allow it, it can also expand you. It can show you that there is more to this life than what you can see or touch, that love does not end, that connection does not disappear, that something exists beyond the physical.

When the Unknown Becomes the Doorway

There is a paradox at the heart of grief: the very thing that feels most terrifying—not knowing—is also the thing that holds the most possibility. When we do not know what comes next, we are forced into the present moment. When we do not have all the answers, we are invited to remain open. And it is in that openness that something unexpected can arrive.

I have met many people who say they wish they could have seen their loss coming. They believe that foreknowledge would have changed things, that they could have prepared, protected, or prevented the unimaginable. But I have come to believe something different. I believe that if I had known what was ahead of me, I might have spent the years before those losses in a state of dread rather than living them. Not knowing allowed me to love fully, without the shadow of what was coming.

This is not a small thing. Love lived fully, without the constant awareness of its impermanence, is perhaps one of the most generous gifts that not knowing has to offer. Of course, there is a grief in that, too. There is grief in learning, after the fact, that you had no idea what was coming. There is a disorientation in looking back on ordinary moments—a Tuesday morning, a shared meal, a conversation you didn't know would be the last—and realizing how much you didn't know. But that disorientation, once you move through it, can become something powerful: a reminder to be present in the moments you still have.

One of the most consistent things I hear from people who are grieving is some version of this: I just want to go back. Back to before. Back to when everything was okay. I understand this longing completely. But I also know that "before" was not always as perfect as grief makes it seem. Grief has a way of gilding the past, of smoothing over the difficulties and illuminating only the beauty. This is not a flaw—it is love asserting itself. But it is worth noticing.

The path forward is not backward. The path forward is into the not knowing—with all the discomfort and possibility that entails. And that path, as difficult as it is, is where transformation waits.

A Note on Courage

Choosing to read a book about grief takes courage. Choosing to feel your grief, rather than bury it, takes courage. Choosing to remain open to the possibility of healing, when part of you would rather shut down, takes courage.

I want to name that clearly, because I think we underestimate how much courage grief demands. We tend to admire physical courage—the kind that involves jumping into danger or standing up in a crowd. But the quieter courage of grief—the courage to keep living, to keep loving, to keep opening your heart after it has been broken—is just as real and just as worthy of recognition.

Reflection: *What has loss changed in you? Not just what it has taken, but what it has revealed. What has it opened? What has it broken? And what might still be waiting for you on the other side of it?*

That discovery is at the heart of this book. And it begins in the not knowing

Chapter 2: Grief Defined

"Grief never really goes away; instead, you learn to integrate the pain into your life."
~ Robin Chodak

Before I can explain what lies beyond grief, I must first define it. Based on my experiences, grief is one of the most misunderstood human experiences and often one of the most difficult to articulate. The dictionary defines grief as "deep mental anguish arising from bereavement," and while that is accurate, it barely scratches the surface. Grief is not just something you think or feel—it is something you experience in your entire being. It is raw, physical, emotional, and consuming. It lives in your body as much as in your heart and mind, born from the severing of a relationship or the loss of someone or something deeply loved.

When I found Steve dead, I felt grief in every fiber of my being. For a long time, I lived with it like an itchy sweater I could not take off. It clung to me, became part of me, followed me everywhere. Grief is not abstract—it is visceral. You feel it through all of your senses. After his death, I became acutely aware of mine. I would hear sounds that reminded me of him, touch his clothes and feel a presence that seemed almost tangible. At times, I could smell him and even taste the memory of his kisses.

Think back to your first kiss. You didn't just experience it emotionally—you experienced it with your entire body. Every sense came alive at once, shaping how you interpreted that moment. You either wanted it to last forever, or you were relieved when it ended. Either way, your senses defined the experience. Grief works the same way. When someone you love dies, your sensory world is disrupted. You no longer see, hear, touch, or feel them as you once did. And sometimes, it can feel as though your senses themselves have gone quiet. That numbness is part of what makes grief such a shock to your body and your soul.

The Science of Grief: What Happens in Your Brain

Grief can make you feel like you are losing your mind. The truth is—you are not. Your brain is responding exactly as it was designed to in the face of overwhelming loss. When someone you love dies—especially in a traumatic way—your body can enter a state of shock. Your head may feel foggy or numb, and you may struggle to process reality. This is not weakness; it is protection. The loss acts as a stressor, triggering your pituitary gland to signal your adrenal glands to release cortisol, the body's primary stress hormone.

During grief, cortisol levels often remain elevated. Over time, this can weaken your immune system, which is why many people become physically ill while grieving. It may also help explain why some elderly spouses pass away not long after their partner. The body, overwhelmed by loss, begins to break down under the weight of prolonged stress. In my own experience, grief showed up as severe backaches and headaches. Your body will speak to you during grief—pay attention to it. It is trying to tell you what it needs.

The emotional center of your brain, including areas like the anterior cingulate cortex, can become underactive during grief. This makes it harder to regulate emotions, which is why something small—like burned toast or a spilled cup of coffee—can bring you to tears. You may experience mood swings, sleep disturbances, or sudden waves of sadness that seem to come from nowhere. Your brain is not malfunctioning—it is recalibrating after loss. At the same time, your brain's fear centers can become overactive. You may begin to fear that something terrible will happen to the people you love. An unanswered phone call can quickly spiral into a worst-case scenario. Before grief, you may not have thought twice about it. After loss, your brain is trying to protect you from being caught off guard again. A helpful way to understand this is through the acronym FEAR: False Evidence Appearing Real. Your mind presents a possibility as if it were a certainty. When a fearful thought arises, gently ask yourself: *Is this actually happening right now? Do I know for certain this will happen?* The answer is almost always no. These thoughts are learned responses—and what is learned can also be unlearned.

While grief can disrupt your brain, it is important to remember that your brain is also wired to heal. There are specific chemicals that influence your mood, often referred to as the "happy chemicals": dopamine, oxytocin, serotonin, and endorphins. Together, they are sometimes called D.O.S.E. These chemicals can be supported in simple, practical ways—getting enough sleep, moving your body, connecting with others, eating well, and allowing yourself to remember moments of love.

Even something as small as a piece of dark chocolate, a walk outside, or a meaningful conversation can begin to shift your internal state. One of the most powerful ways to support these chemicals is through human connection. Hugging, in particular, has been shown to increase oxytocin levels, helping reduce feelings of loneliness, anxiety, and isolation. It can calm your nervous system, strengthen your immune response, and create a sense of safety.

I have always been a hugger. My daughter will tell you I have hugged strangers in airports after heartfelt conversations. There is something deeply healing about that exchange—both people give and receive at the same time. In grief, those small moments of connection matter more than you may realize. They remind you that you are still here, still capable of giving and receiving love.

Grief can also impact the executive functioning of your brain, located in the prefrontal cortex—the area responsible for rational thinking, decision-making, and impulse control. When it is compromised, you may find yourself reaching for anything that promises relief—food, alcohol, shopping, distraction. These urges can feel convincing, even necessary. But they often provide only temporary escape, not true healing. Too much of anything becomes its own form of suffering.

The encouraging truth is that your brain is not fixed. Through neuroplasticity, it has the ability to change, adapt, and rewire itself—even after trauma. I have experienced this in my own life, and I have seen it in the lives of many clients. Healing is not only possible—it is supported by the very structure of your brain.

There are many ways to support this process: exposing yourself to new experiences, learning something unfamiliar, reading, creating, moving your body, and prioritizing rest. Even small changes—like using your non-dominant hand or trying a new activity—can begin to form new neural pathways. Practices like mindfulness can also help strengthen your brain's ability to regulate emotion and reduce impulsive reactions. Your brain is an extraordinary organ. It deserves your care and attention, especially during grief.

The Many Faces of Grief

Grief itself has many faces. It is not a single emotion but a complex, layered experience that can include sadness, anger, confusion, fear, guilt, numbness, and even moments of unexpected peace. It can leave you feeling disconnected from your life, as though everything you once knew has shifted or disappeared. While grief is a natural response to loss, it can make life feel unfamiliar and, at times, unrecognizable.

One of the most difficult emotions within grief is guilt. It has a way of attaching itself to the past, convincing you that you could have done something differently. Many people replay moments over and over, searching for a version of events where the outcome changed. If you have felt this, you are not alone. But it is important to recognize that guilt can distort reality and erode your sense of self. Left unexamined, it can keep you trapped in a moment that no longer exists.

Some traditions refer to these lingering emotional imprints as samskaras—impressions stored in your body that influence how you see and respond to the world. Whether you use that language or not, the experience is real. Healing requires gently bringing those moments into awareness and allowing them to move through you rather than define you.

Grief is not limited to death. It can arise from divorce, illness, financial hardship, broken relationships, or any significant life change. Loss, in all its forms, has the power to reshape your identity and your understanding of the world.

The Healing Power of Writing

Part of my own healing came through writing. After Steve died, I began writing letters to him. At the time, I did not fully understand why—it was simply something I felt compelled to do. It became a way to release the thoughts and emotions I could not carry alone. Looking back, I now understand that journaling gave my grief a voice. It allowed me to process what felt unprocessable.

One letter, written on August 6, 2006, still stands out to me. In it, I asked questions I didn't know how to answer. I expressed love, longing, and a deep desire to move forward, even though I had no idea how. That letter did not change everything overnight—but it marked the beginning of a shift. Something inside me softened. Something began to open.

A few weeks later, a friend suggested I try Argentine tango. At first, the idea felt impossible. How could I dance when I could barely breathe under the weight of grief? But something in me said yes. And that one decision led me into a new chapter of my life—one filled with connection, movement, and eventually, love again.

When Gerry came into my life, I experienced a kind of happiness I did not think was possible after loss. Our life together was full—of dance, travel, laughter, and shared joy. And then, in 2019, I found myself facing loss again when he died suddenly in our home from an aneurysm. Experiencing that level of loss twice could have broken me completely.

For a long time, I believed I was a target of grief. But over time, my perspective began to shift. I started to see that grief was not something happening to me—it was something working within me.

Today, I no longer see grief as my enemy. I see it as a teacher and, in many ways, a friend. That may sound difficult to accept, especially if you are in the early stages of loss. But consider what a true friend does. A true friend tells you the truth, stands beside you, and wants you to grow. Grief, in its own way, does the same. It brings forward what is unresolved. It reveals what needs healing. And if you allow it, it can guide you toward a deeper understanding of yourself and your life.

Complicated Grief and Post-Traumatic Growth

For some, grief after trauma can develop into post-traumatic stress disorder (PTSD), including intrusive memories, avoidance, emotional numbness, and heightened reactivity. These responses are not signs of weakness—they are natural reactions to overwhelming events. If these symptoms persist or interfere with your ability to function, seeking professional support is essential. Healing does not mean doing it alone.

There is also another possibility—one that is less often discussed but equally real. It is called post-traumatic growth (PTG). This is the process of experiencing positive transformation after profound loss. It does not mean the pain disappears. It means something new begins to emerge alongside it.

Growth can show up as a deeper appreciation for life, stronger relationships, new possibilities, personal strength, or spiritual expansion. I have experienced this firsthand. But growth does not happen by accident. It requires a willingness to shift your perspective, to question old beliefs, and to remain open to change. For me, that shift began the moment I stood on the beach and asked for my thoughts to be taken away. When my mind quieted, something new had space to enter. That was the beginning of a different way of living—my transformation.

The Practice of Gratitude

Practices like gratitude can also support this transformation. Gratitude does not deny pain—it exists alongside it. In my darkest moments, I began focusing on the smallest things: a warm bed, a kind word, the presence of family. I was especially grateful for the birth of my granddaughter just days before Steve's death. Even in the midst of loss, there was still life.

Over time, those small moments of gratitude began to shift my perspective. Research supports this—gratitude can improve emotional well-being, sleep, resilience, and overall happiness. Simple practices, like keeping a gratitude journal or pausing to acknowledge something meaningful each day, can begin to rewire how you experience your life.

If you are not currently keeping a gratitude journal, I encourage you to start today. You do not need to list ten things or write paragraphs. Begin with one. One true thing you are grateful for, however small. A warm cup of coffee. The sound of rain. A text from someone who loves you.

These moments are real. And over time, they accumulate into something that can sustain you.

Grief is complex. It lives in your body, your brain, your senses, and your spirit all at once. But the more you begin to understand what it is and how it moves through you, the less powerless you feel.

In the chapters ahead, we will move beyond defining grief and begin exploring what lies beyond it—because there is something there. And it is more beautiful than you might imagine.

Types of Loss and How They Shape Grief

Before we move forward, I want to acknowledge something that is often overlooked in discussions about grief: not all loss is the same. The grief that follows the death of a spouse is not identical to the grief that follows the death of a child, or a parent, or a sibling, or a close friend. And the grief that follows a sudden, violent death is different from the grief that comes at the end of a long illness. All of it is real. All of it is valid. But understanding the particular nature of your loss can help you be more compassionate with yourself as you move through it.

When a spouse dies, there is a unique combination of losses: the loss of a companion, a witness to your life, a partner in the practical tasks of living, and often the primary source of intimacy and belonging. The world reorganizes in fundamental ways. You may find yourself suddenly alone in a bed, or at a dinner table, or in a car, in ways that feel unbearable in their ordinariness. The small, daily reminders of absence can sometimes be harder to bear than the large, formal moments of grief.

When a child dies, the loss carries a particular anguish that has no adequate words. It violates what feels like the natural order of things—parents are not supposed to outlive their children. The grief of a bereaved parent carries with it not just the loss of a person, but the loss of a future. A future full of milestones and moments that will never be. If you have experienced this kind of loss, I want you to know that there is support specifically designed for you, and that your grief, which can feel unlike anything others around you understand, is not something you have to carry alone.

When a parent dies, the grief can be complicated by the length of the relationship, by unresolved history, by the natural shifting of roles that aging creates, and sometimes by relief when death follows a long period of illness. If you have felt relief alongside grief, please know that this is not a betrayal of your love. It is a natural human response to watching someone suffer. Relief and grief can coexist and feeling one does not diminish the other.

When a sibling dies, you lose not just a person but a witness to your shared history. A sibling carries memories that no one else holds—memories of your childhood, your family, your origins. When they are gone, those memories become something you hold alone. That is a particular kind of loneliness that is not always recognized by the outside world.

There is also the grief of losing someone to suicide, which I have spoken of before and will return to again because it deserves acknowledgment. Suicide grief carries unique layers: shock, horror, guilt, confusion, anger, and a profound sense of having missed something. Survivors often replay conversations and moments, searching for what they might have seen or said or done differently. If you are in this particular grief, please hear me: you did not fail them. And you deserve the same compassion you would offer to anyone else who is suffering.

Finally, there is the grief that does not involve death at all—the grief of divorce, of estrangement, of the end of a friendship, of a diagnosis that changes your life, of a dream you had to let go. These losses are real, and the grief they produce is real, even when the world does not give them the same weight as death. If you find yourself grieving something that others do not recognize as a loss, please trust your experience. Grief is grief. It does not require a death certificate to be valid.

Grief and Identity

One of the most disorienting aspects of grief—particularly grief after the death of a spouse or long-term partner—is the way it disrupts your sense of identity. For many people, who they are has been inseparable from who they are with. When that person is gone, the question of *who am I now* can feel genuinely unanswerable.

I experienced this acutely after Steve died. I had been Robin and Steve for so long that Robin alone felt incomplete. I didn't know how to fill a room by myself. I didn't know how to tell my own story without referencing his. I had to, in some fundamental sense, learn who I was as an individual again—and at a time when I had very little energy for that kind of excavation.

If you are experiencing this, I want to offer you something that helped me. The identity you had within your relationship is not lost—it is part of you. The love you gave, the ways you grew, the person you became because of that relationship—all of that is yours. It does not leave with them. It remains, woven into who you are, and it will continue to shape who you become.

Identity after loss is not about becoming someone new. It is about discovering the fullness of who you already are, now that you are navigating the world in a different configuration. This can, over time, become one of grief's most unexpected gifts: a deeper, more honest relationship with yourself than you may have had before.

Grief and the Body: Physical Practices for Healing

Throughout this chapter, I have touched on the ways grief lives in the body. I want to close with some specific, practical suggestions for supporting your body during the grief process, because your body is not just a passive vessel for your emotional experience—it is an active participant in your healing.

Movement is one of the most powerful tools available to you. I know that when you are in the depths of grief, the idea of exercise can feel absurd. But movement—even gentle, slow movement—has been shown to reduce cortisol levels, increase the happy chemicals we discussed earlier, and improve sleep, mood, and resilience. You do not need to join a gym or commit to a rigorous routine. A walk around the block, a few gentle stretches in the morning or dancing alone in your kitchen to a song that matters to you are not frivolous activities—they are medicine.

For me, Argentine tango became a lifeline after Steve died. There was something about the physical act of moving with another person, of trusting and being trusted, of giving and receiving—that began to heal something in me that words could not reach. Dance reconnected me to my body at a time when I had retreated deep inside my head. It did not take away the grief, but it gave the grief somewhere to go.

Sleep is also critical, and grief frequently disrupts it. The intrusive thoughts, the heightened anxiety, the emotional exhaustion that paradoxically prevents rest—all of these can combine to create a cycle of sleep deprivation that makes everything harder. If you are struggling with sleep, please treat it as a priority, not an afterthought. Speak to your doctor if necessary. Explore practices like gentle yoga before bed, limiting screens in the evening, and creating a sleep environment that feels safe and comforting.

Nutrition matters as well. Grief often suppresses appetite or drives you toward the kinds of foods that feel comforting in the moment but deplete you over time. This is not a judgment—grief is hard, and if a bowl of ice cream gets you through a difficult evening, that is okay. But as best you can, try to nourish yourself with food that supports your body. Your brain and your body need fuel to heal and denying them that fuel makes an already difficult process harder.

Finally, seek physical touch. Hugging, as I mentioned earlier, increases oxytocin and reduces feelings of isolation. If you live alone and are not getting regular human contact, this is something worth actively addressing. A massage. A visit with a friend who is a good hugger. A pet, whose comfort is scientifically measurable and deeply real. Do not underestimate the healing power of being touched by someone who cares.

Reflection: *What type of loss are you navigating, and how does its specific nature shape your grief? How has loss affected your sense of who you are? What does your body most need right now in order to heal? Are there movement, sleep, or nourishment practices you could begin this week?*

Chapter 3: What Is Death?

"It is not death that a man should fear, but he should fear never beginning to live."
~ Marcus Aurelius

I have talked at length about grief, and now it is time to talk about death. There would be no discussion of what lies beyond if death did not exist. *Do you avoid the topic of death? If* so, you are not alone. It makes most people uncomfortable. There is a quiet uneasiness that surrounds it, often rooted in one simple truth—we do not know what it is like. And as human beings, we tend to fear what we cannot understand.

Some people even believe that speaking about death somehow invites it closer. While that fear is understandable, it can keep us from one of the most important conversations we will ever have—with ourselves. Death comes to all of us, each in its own time. It is woven into the very fabric of life. And yet, despite its certainty, we spend much of our lives avoiding it. There is also another kind of death—one that does not happen in a single moment but unfolds slowly over time. It occurs when you surrender your power, allow others to dictate your life, or engage in habits that quietly erode your health and spirit. It is the slow fading of aliveness, and in many ways, it is the one we have the most control over.

Avoiding death as a topic comes at a cost. When you allow yourself to reflect on your own impermanence, something begins to shift. You start to see time differently. You become more aware of the moments you are living—and the ones you are letting pass you by. You have a heart that beats, a mind that thinks, a body that moves. You can feel, love, connect, laugh, and experience life in real time. And yet, so many of us hold back.

For many people, loss becomes the doorway into this awareness. It opens conversations about death that would otherwise never happen. And surprisingly, those conversations are not always as heavy as we expect them to be. They can feel grounding. Even comforting. They can invite the possibility that something exists beyond what we can see. Whether or not you know what happens after death, considering it has the power to change how you live now.

What We Miss

I do not believe the deceased experience grief in the way we do. It is those of us who remain who feel its weight.

Grief is painful because it disrupts the shared experiences that once defined your relationship. All relationships are built on moments—conversations, touch, laughter, presence. These moments are experienced through your senses: what you see, hear, feel, taste, and smell.

When someone dies, those sensory connections are suddenly gone. And that absence is what cuts so deeply. I missed watching Ralene cheer at football games and hearing her excitement about becoming a hairdresser. I missed listening to Steve play his guitar, watching baseball together, and sharing something as simple as French fries. I missed the warmth of Gerry's arms as we danced, the rhythm of tango, the joy of traveling, and the quiet moments we shared.

Take a moment to reflect on what you miss most. Not to deepen your pain—but to honor the love that created those memories. Because death does not erase love. The people we lose continue to live within us—in our thoughts, our choices, and the way we move through the world.

What Happens After Death?

Grief is intense because love is real. And if love continues, it is only natural to wonder—what happens to the person who is no longer here? The truth is, we do not fully know. Science has not yet provided a definitive answer. But that has never stopped us from asking the question. Near-death experiences, spiritual traditions, and personal beliefs all offer different perspectives.

Some believe in rebirth. Some believe in an afterlife. Some believe consciousness continues in a form we cannot yet understand. I have learned to hold this question with openness rather than needing certainty. Today, I believe that those we love continue to exist in some form—beyond the physical body. Whether you think of that as energy, spirit, or something else entirely, there is a scientific principle that offers a quiet kind of comfort: energy cannot be created or destroyed; it can only change form.
That idea has brought me peace—not as proof, but as possibility. A possibility that allows love to continue.

Perhaps death is not an ending, but a transition. Perhaps it is something far greater than we can currently comprehend. We do not remember the moment we entered this world. It is possible we will not remember the moment we leave it either. And maybe that is not something to fear.

Near-Death Experiences and What They Suggest

For centuries, people who have come close to death and returned have described remarkably similar experiences: a feeling of leaving the body, moving through a tunnel of light, encountering deceased loved ones, and feeling an overwhelming sense of peace and love. These accounts span cultures, religions, and time periods, suggesting something that is difficult to dismiss as coincidence or purely neurological.

Dr. Raymond Moody, who coined the term "near-death experience" in his 1975 book *Life After Life*, documented dozens of such accounts. What struck him was not just the consistency across different individuals, but the profound and lasting transformation these experiences produced. People who had been terrified of death returned from these episodes with an almost complete absence of fear. They described feeling more love, more compassion, and more clarity about what truly mattered in life.

I am not suggesting that near-death experiences are proof of what lies beyond. Science has offered several explanations—oxygen deprivation, the release of endorphins, REM intrusion—and these deserve serious consideration. I do think they are worth acknowledging, because they are experienced as profoundly real by the people who live them. And when someone returns from the edge of death transformed, that transformation is itself a kind of evidence that something significant occurred.

More recently, researchers like Dr. Pim van Lommel, a Dutch cardiologist, have studied near-death experiences in controlled settings with cardiac arrest patients. His work, published in the medical journal *The Lancet*, found that a significant percentage of patients reported consciousness continuing even when brain activity had flatlined. He concluded that current neuroscience cannot fully account for these experiences, and that consciousness may be more than simply a product of brain function.

I share this not to push any particular belief, but to open a door. If you have wondered whether your loved one might still exist in some form—whether the love you shared might have somewhere to go after death—you are not alone in that wondering. Some of the most rigorous scientists and scholars on the planet are wondering the same thing.

Cultural and Spiritual Perspectives on Death

Different cultures and spiritual traditions have approached death in vastly different ways and exploring them can be surprisingly comforting. In many Indigenous traditions, death is understood as a transition rather than an ending. The deceased are believed to remain present in the community—in the land, in the wind, in the stories told about them. They are spoken to, honored in ceremony, and understood as continuing participants in the life of the living.

In Hinduism, death is seen as the shedding of the physical body, while the soul continues its journey through multiple lifetimes. The Bhagavad Gita describes the soul as eternal and unchanging: it is never born and it never dies. This perspective transforms death from a final ending into a single transition in a much longer story.

In many African spiritual traditions, ancestors are considered active members of the family even after death. They are consulted, invoked, and honored as living presences who continue to protect and guide the living.

Across the African diaspora—in practices like Vodou, Candomblé, and Santeria—maintaining a relationship with the deceased is not considered unusual or delusional. It is considered essential. Even in Western Christianity, where death is often framed in terms of heaven and hell, the belief in resurrection and eternal life carries a similar thread: love does not end. Connection does not end. The soul continues. I find it meaningful that so many different cultures, across so many centuries, have arrived at some version of the same conclusion: the dead are not entirely gone. They are simply elsewhere. And something in the living reaches toward them.

If you have been taught to dismiss that reaching as grief-induced delusion, I want to gently offer another possibility. Perhaps it is instinct. Perhaps it is knowledge that lives deeper than what we have been taught to understand.

Reflecting on Death

When you begin to think about death, it can shift how you experience life. I invite you to sit with a few simple questions:

Reflection: *Does thinking about death make you uncomfortable? What do you believe death is? How often do you think about it? What brings it to mind? And does thinking about it change how you live?*

There are no right or wrong answers—only your answers. For me, thinking about death no longer brings fear in the way it once did. It brings awareness. It reminds me that life is finite, and therefore meaningful. It strengthens my desire to live fully and to help others do the same.

When Steve died, I searched desperately for answers. I asked *why* over and over again, hoping something would make sense. Over time, I came to understand that some questions do not have answers we can access. And in that acceptance, I found a measure of peace.

When Gerry died years later, the experience was different. His passing was peaceful, and that contrast shifted something within me. It led me to consider that death is not always filled with fear or pain. In some cases, it may be quiet. Even gentle. These experiences taught me something simple, yet profound: while we cannot control death, we can choose how we live.

The Art of Saying Goodbye

One of the things that makes death so complicated is that we rarely have the chance to say goodbye in the way we might choose. Some deaths are sudden—a call in the night, an accident, a heart attack—and there is no preparation, no last conversation, no opportunity for closure. Other deaths unfold slowly, and even then, there may be things left unspoken.

If you are carrying the weight of words unsaid, I want to address that directly. Perhaps you never told them how much they meant to you. Perhaps there was a conflict that was never resolved. Perhaps the last words you exchanged were not the words you wish had been your last. If any of this resonates, please know that you are not alone. It is one of the most common sources of prolonged grief, and it is one that can be addressed, even now.

You can say what you need to say—now, in a letter, in a quiet moment of connection. The conversation is not over simply because they are no longer physically present to hear your words. I have spoken directly to Steve, to Gerry, and to Ralene about things that went unsaid during their lifetimes. These were not performances for my own benefit.

They were genuine communications, offered with the belief that love, and intention can cross whatever boundary death creates.

If you have unfinished business with someone who has died—things you needed to hear from them, or to say to them—consider speaking those words out loud, or writing them in a letter, and trusting that they will find their way. I cannot prove they do. But I have felt, in my own experience, something that feels very much like resolution when I have done it. And that feeling of resolution is worth pursuing.

You can also work with a therapist or a coach like me who specializes in grief to process the more complicated emotions that unfinished conversations can produce.

Techniques that I teach like empty chair work—in which you speak to an empty chair representing the person who died—have helped many people access and process emotions that have otherwise felt stuck. There is no single right way to reach resolution. There is only your way, taken with intention and care.

Living with the Questions

One of the most important lessons that grief has taught me is how to live with questions I cannot answer. *What happens after death? Why did this happen? What is the meaning of a life cut short? Is there a plan, or is existence random and indifferent?*

These are not trivial questions. They are some of the most profound questions human beings ever ask. And the honest answer is that we do not know. Not fully. Not with certainty.

For a long time, I found that not knowing felt unbearable. I wanted answers. I wanted to understand. I thought that if I could just make sense of what happened, the pain would ease. But sense-making, I eventually discovered, is not always available. Sometimes things happen that do not resolve into meaning, no matter how long or how hard you search.

What changed for me was not finding answers. It was developing a different relationship with the questions. Instead of needing to resolve them, I began to hold them with curiosity rather than despair. Instead of being frightened by the not-knowing, I began to see it as a form of openness—a space where something unexpected might still arrive.

This is, in fact, the posture of the 7th stage of grief. It is not a posture of certainty. It is a posture of openness. Of willingness. Of trust that love and connection are real, even when they cannot be fully explained. If you are in a season of unanswerable questions, I want you to know that you do not need to resolve them in order to heal. You need only to carry them gently, without letting them become anchors. You can live, fully and meaningfully, while holding the mystery of death alongside the reality of your life.

Impermanence

Death reminds us that nothing in this life is permanent. At first, that realization can feel unsettling. But over time, it can become one of life's greatest teachers.

Everything changes—your emotions, your circumstances, your thoughts, even your identity. And that includes your grief. What feels unbearable today will not always feel that way. Understanding impermanence helped me survive my darkest moments. It reminded me that no feeling lasts forever. That even the deepest pain will shift, soften, and eventually transform.

It also creates a quiet urgency—not rooted in fear, but in meaning. If life is temporary, then each moment matters. Each connection matters. Each choice matters. Time itself is shaped by perception. It moves quickly when you are engaged in life and slows when you are in pain. This is your reminder to be present for the moments that matter—because they are the only ones you truly have.

I will leave you with this: You are going to die. It may be tomorrow or decades from now—but it is inevitable. Not as something to fear, but as something to understand. So, the question becomes: *what will you do with the time you have? Will you hold back? Or will you begin to truly live?* Knowing that life is finite is not meant to scare you. It is meant to set you free.

Chapter 4: Pain and Suffering

"The truth that many people never understand until it is too late is that the more you try to avoid suffering, the more you suffer."
~ Thomas Merton

Pain is a physical, mental, or emotional experience. If you break your arm, you feel physical pain from the injury. It is uncomfortable—sometimes intense—but it eventually subsides. Once the cast comes off, you don't spend your days reliving the moment it happened. You move forward. You use your arm again.

Emotional pain, however, does not always follow the same path. Especially when it is tied to loss, it can linger. Instead of fading, it can replay itself over and over, quietly embedding into your daily life. When that happens, pain can evolve into something deeper—something heavier. It becomes suffering.

Suffering is different from pain, and the distinction matters. Pain is the event or experience itself. Suffering is your relationship to it. One is something that happens to you. The other is something that develops over time, shaped by your thoughts, your beliefs, and the meaning you assign to what has happened.

After Steve died, I felt as though the pain would never end. It lived in every cell of my body. I felt frozen in time, unable to move forward. Fear took hold of my thoughts, and I became afraid to leave my house. I was no longer just grieving—I was stuck. Looking back, I can see that this "stuckness" became my suffering. The pain was real and unavoidable, but the way I held onto it kept me trapped inside it.

What I know now is something I could not see then: those emotions, as overwhelming as they felt, were not permanent. They moved through me, even when I believed they never would. And for that, I am deeply grateful. There is a teaching often attributed to the Buddha that says *pain is inevitable, but suffering is optional.* At first, that idea can feel impossible—especially if you are in the depths of grief. But over time, it begins to make sense. Pain is part of being human. Loss will always hurt. But suffering is influenced by how long we stay in that pain, how tightly we hold onto it, and what we begin to believe because of it.

When Gerry died, I experienced grief again—but I responded differently. Not because I loved him any less, but because I had grown. I had learned how to move through pain without allowing it to consume me. I made choices that supported my healing rather than prolonging my suffering. That shift changed everything.

The Roots of Suffering

Loss of any kind—whether it is a person, a relationship, or a life you once imagined—can bring emotional pain. But that pain does not have to define the rest of your life. Suffering often takes root beneath the surface, fueled by beliefs you may not even realize you are carrying.

Thoughts like *I am not good enough* or *I don't deserve happiness* can quietly anchor you in place. If you find yourself unable to move forward, gently begin to examine what lies underneath your pain. What are you telling yourself about what happened? What meaning have you attached to it? You have more influence over your internal world than you may realize. And with awareness, those patterns can begin to shift.

One of the most important things I have learned in my work as a grief coach is that suffering often contains a hidden story—a narrative we have created to explain our pain, and one that we then begin to live inside of without realizing it. The story might be: This happened because I wasn't enough. Or: If only I had done something differently. Or: I will never be happy again. These stories feel like truth. They feel like facts. But they are not facts. They are interpretations, and interpretations can be gently questioned and, over time, revised.

This does not mean denying your pain or forcing yourself to feel something you don't. It means becoming curious about the story you are telling—and asking whether that story is truly serving your healing, or whether it is keeping you in a place that is no longer necessary. You have the right to experience joy again. You have the right to live fully. Please do not allow suffering to become a lifelong companion when it does not have to be.

The Judgment of Others

There is another layer to suffering that is often overlooked—the fear of being judged. Not for your loss, but for how you move through it.

In my coaching work, I have seen how often people feel pressure to grieve in a certain way or for a certain length of time. If someone begins to smile again, to laugh, or to re-engage with life sooner than expected, others may question the depth of their love. This belief is not only inaccurate—it is harmful.

Love is not measured by how long you suffer. It is not proven by how deeply you remain in pain. Love continues in many forms, long after physical presence is gone. People judge for many reasons—discomfort, lack of understanding, fear of their own grief, or simply not knowing what to say. But their opinions do not define your experience. You are not here to grieve according to someone else's expectations. Your path through loss is yours alone. And however you choose to walk it is valid.

When Grief Becomes Complicated

It is worth noting that some grief does not follow an expected trajectory and requires additional support. Complicated grief—sometimes called prolonged grief disorder—is a form of intense grief that interferes significantly with daily functioning over an extended period. It may involve an inability to accept the death, intense longing that does not ease over time, difficulty engaging in normal activities, or feeling that life has no meaning without the person who died.

If this sounds familiar, please know that it does not mean you are broken or beyond help. It means you may benefit from working with a grief counselor, therapist, or coach who specializes in loss. Complicated grief can be treated, and people do recover from it. Asking for help is an act of courage, not failure.

There is also something important to say about grief after suicide. Losing someone to suicide creates a unique and particularly complex form of grief. The shock is often profound. The questions are often unanswerable. The guilt can be overwhelming. And the stigma—though it is slowly diminishing—can create isolation at precisely the time when connection is most needed.

I know this from personal experience. Steve's death changed me in ways I am still understanding. It also gave me a mission: to show others who are walking this particular road that healing is possible. That you can survive this. That the love you had for the person you lost is not contaminated by the manner of their death. That you deserve support, and that asking for it is one of the most important things you can do.

Inner Peace

As you begin to move through grief, something important starts to emerge—a deeper understanding of what truly brings you peace. Not temporary relief. Not distraction. But real, lasting peace.

Have you ever asked yourself what that is for you? If the answer is not clear, that is okay. This is an invitation to explore. To pause. To listen to yourself in a way you may not have before. Often, what is missing in our lives becomes most visible in moments of loss.

Inner peace does not come from changing your circumstances. It comes from how you relate to them—how you think, how you feel, and how you respond to what is in front of you.

Letting Go of Control

Time has often been compared to a river—you cannot touch the same water twice. Once a moment passes, it is gone. And yet, many of us spend our lives trying to hold onto what was. We replay the past, trying to recreate what felt good, or to change what did not. We attempt to control outcomes, to shape life into something predictable and safe. But control is an illusion. And more often than not, it keeps you stuck.

Living fully requires something different. It asks for trust. Trust in yourself, in your ability to navigate what comes, and—if it resonates with you—in something greater than yourself. Whether you call it God, Spirit, or simply life unfolding, there is a flow to existence that cannot be forced.

Letting go is not giving up. It is allowing. It is choosing to participate in life as it is, rather than resisting it at every turn. And in that allowing, something begins to shift. Space opens. Possibility returns.

> **Reflection:** *What truly brings you inner peace? Where in your life are you holding onto pain in a way that has become suffering? And where might you be gripping so tightly that you are missing what is right in front of you?*

Write your answers down. They may reveal more than you expect.

The Role of Forgiveness in Healing

There is one more element of suffering that I feel compelled to address before we move on: forgiveness. Not because it is simple, but because its absence can become one of the most persistent sources of prolonged suffering. When someone dies, there is sometimes a need to forgive them. For things they said or did not say. For the way they lived, or the way they died. For leaving. This may sound strange—it can feel wrong to be angry at someone who is gone, or to feel that forgiveness is needed. But grief has its own logic, and the emotions that arise within it do not always follow the rules of what seems appropriate.

After Steve died by suicide, I was angry. I was terrified to admit that, even to myself, because it felt like a betrayal of my love for him. But the anger was real. I felt abandoned. I felt confused. I felt a kind of fury at the circumstances that had brought us to that moment. And beneath the fury was a grief so deep it had no bottom. Forgiveness, in that context, was not something that happened quickly or completely. It was something I worked toward, slowly and imperfectly, over years. Not because Steve deserved to be released from some imagined accountability, but because I needed to be released from the weight of carrying resentment alongside grief. Forgiveness is, ultimately, something we do for ourselves.

Many grieving people carry a burden of self-blame that is crushing. They believe they should have seen it coming, should have done something differently, should have called more often, should have been better. If you are carrying this, I want to say to you directly: you did what you knew how to do, with what you had, at the time you had it. That is all any of us can do. Punishing yourself now, in the present, for what you did not know or could not do in the past, serves no one—not you, and not the person you lost.

Forgiveness does not mean that what happened was okay. It means you are willing to release the grip of resentment or shame so that it no longer has the power to define your present. It is one of the most profound acts of self-care available to a grieving person, and it is available to you, however long the road to it may be.

Finding Professional Support

I want to take a moment to speak directly about professional support, because I believe in it deeply and because I have seen many people trying to navigate profound loss entirely alone. Therapy, counseling, and grief coaching are not signs of weakness. They are signs of wisdom—an acknowledgment that what you are carrying is heavy, that you deserve support, and that healing is important enough to invest in. I have worked with therapists, grief counselors, coaches, and support groups throughout my own grief journey. Each offered something different. Each contributed to my healing in ways I could not have achieved on my own.

If you have not yet sought professional support, I encourage you to consider it. This is particularly important if you are experiencing symptoms of complicated grief, PTSD, or depression—or if you feel that your grief is not shifting over time. There are people like me who are trained specifically to help you move through loss, and there is no reason to power through on your own when someone can help you navigate with more grace and less pain.

Chapter 5: What Are Signs?

"The world is full of magic things, patiently waiting for our senses to grow sharper."
~ W.B. Yeats

I must explain the meaning of signs so that you can begin to recognize them in your own life—especially as you move into the deeper stages of grief. Signs appear in many forms: an object, a feeling, a moment, or an event whose presence suggests something beyond the ordinary. They may come from deceased loved ones or from a realm we do not fully understand. However they arrive, their purpose is often the same—to guide, reassure, or remind you that you are not alone. Sometimes they appear as symbols that hold deep personal meaning. Other times, they show up quietly—subtle at first, but persistent enough to make you pause. The truth is that signs are not rare. They are everywhere. The question is whether you are open enough to notice them.

I believe that connections exist between the physical and non-physical worlds—whether you call that God, Spirit, higher consciousness, or something else entirely. These connections often reveal themselves through signs. The challenge is not that signs are absent. It is that we frequently overlook them, dismiss them, or forget them too quickly. That is why I have made it a practice to journal about these moments or share them with someone I trust while they are still fresh. What follows are some of my own experiences. I do not share them to convince you of anything. I share them so that you may begin to notice your own.

The Paranormal Morning

On November 2, 2022, I was in my kitchen making coffee, speaking aloud to Gerry as I often do. His picture sits next to my coffee maker, and our conversations have become part of my daily ritual. That morning, I asked him to watch over my health—I had been battling a respiratory virus for weeks—and to look after my mother, who was undergoing treatment for a malignant tumor.

As a physician, Gerry always had a calming presence. I found myself asking for that reassurance again. I then asked my Amazon Alexa device to play NPR news, something I do every morning. Instead of responding normally, Alexa began spelling out letters: P-A-R-A-N. Assuming it was a glitch, I asked again. The same response. Slightly frustrated, I raised my voice and tried a third time. Slowly, deliberately, the full word appeared on the screen: P-A-R-A-N-O-R-M-A-L.

I stood there, coffee in hand, completely still.
Why would a simple request for the news produce that word? I do not believe it was random. I experienced it as a response—as if Gerry were acknowledging me, reminding me that he exists beyond what I can see, and that the connection I was reaching for was real. My reaction was immediate and heartfelt: "Thank you, Gerry."

That moment led me to explore the concept of the paranormal more deeply. The word itself refers to events beyond what is considered normal—experiences that cannot yet be explained by science. While popular culture often portrays these ideas as fiction, many people quietly experience moments that feel just as real.

Have you ever misplaced something only to find it later in an unlikely place? Or had something long lost suddenly reappear? Moments like these are easy to dismiss—but they are also worth noticing.

Extrasensory Perception and Oak Park

Extrasensory perception—often called ESP—is the ability to perceive something beyond the five physical senses. It can show up as intuition, a sudden knowing, or a feeling that cannot be logically explained.

I experienced this in 1990, shortly after my divorce. At the time, I had rarely ventured beyond the Chicago suburb where I had spent most of my life. One day, feeling drawn toward something new, a friend and I visited Oak Park—an artsy, vibrant community I had never explored. As I walked through the streets, I was suddenly overcome with a strong and undeniable feeling: I would live there one day. There was no logical reason for this. No plan. No connection. And yet, the knowing was clear and complete.

Five years later, I met Steve. We married and eventually bought a home in Oak Park. That moment had been a glimpse—a sign that arrived before its time.
If you have ever experienced something like that—a knowing that made no sense until later—you may already be more intuitive than you realize.

Steve, Music, and 11:11

After Steve died, I could not listen to the music we had shared. Songs that once brought joy became too painful to hear. I would turn them off immediately. Then one day, something shifted. A song came on, and for the first time, I let it play. When it ended, I glanced at the clock. It read 11:11.

The next day, it happened again. And then again. Soon, I began seeing 11:11 everywhere—on clocks, appliances, screens—often at moments that felt connected to him. I could not ignore the pattern.

Whether you view numbers symbolically or not, repetition has a way of getting your attention. For me, each time I saw it, I felt a sense of connection—as though Steve was reaching through in a way I could understand.

When I later shared these experiences with Gerry, he was initially skeptical. As a man of science, it challenged his worldview. But over time, as he witnessed patterns in his own life, his perspective softened. It was ultimately one of the reasons he agreed to marry on 11/11/11—a date that now holds deep meaning for me.

Rather than dismissing these moments as coincidence, I chose to experience them as connection. And that choice brought me comfort.

The Concert Experience

In 2017, I felt an unexpected pull to attend a Doors tribute concert. I could not explain why, but I trusted the feeling and went. Gerry came with me.

During the performance, something happened that I still cannot fully explain. As I stood near the stage, immersed in the music, I closed my eyes. When I opened them, I saw Steve—clear as day—standing beside what appeared to be Jim Morrison. He was playing guitar exactly as I remembered him. I blinked, and the moment passed. Was it a hallucination? Perhaps. But I was fully present, and what I felt in that moment was not fear—it was joy. It felt like a gift.

Whether you interpret that experience as psychological, spiritual, or something else entirely, its impact was real. It brought me comfort, connection, and a sense that love continues in ways we do not yet fully understand.

Signs in Everyday Life

Signs do not always arrive in dramatic ways. More often, they appear in ordinary moments—through conversations, timing, or events that align just a little too perfectly to ignore.

I have experienced this in airports, on airplanes, through songs that play at exactly the right moment, and even through small disruptions—like a broken lamp that carried a message I needed to hear. These moments share something in common: they arrive when you need them most.

I want to offer you a few ways to begin cultivating your own awareness of signs, because the ability to receive them is not something reserved for the few. It is something available to anyone who is willing to pay attention.
The first practice is simply noticing. Before you decide whether something is a sign, notice it. Notice the song that played when you were thinking about your loved one. Notice the animal that stopped and looked at you. Notice the number that appeared at precisely the right moment. You do not need to explain it or defend it to anyone. You simply need to notice it.

The second practice is recording. I cannot emphasize this enough. Write it down. The mind is busy, and small miracles are easy to forget. A brief note in your phone, a sentence in your journal—whatever works for you. Over time, what began as isolated moments begin to reveal themselves as a pattern. And patterns are harder to dismiss than individual events.

The third practice is sharing. When you share a meaningful experience with someone who is also open, something is reinforced—not just the memory, but your trust in your own perception. Find at least one person in your life with whom you can speak honestly about these moments without fear of being dismissed. If no one immediately comes to mind, consider joining a grief support group where these experiences are welcomed rather than pathologized.

Dreams as Signs

Dreams are another powerful way signs can reach you. Every night, your mind enters a different state—one where logic softens and deeper awareness can emerge. Many people report dreaming of loved ones who have passed, often describing the experience as vivid, peaceful, and real. Have you ever had a dream that stayed with you long after you woke up? One that felt different from the rest? Those dreams are worth paying attention to.

If you want to remember your dreams more clearly, try setting an intention before you fall asleep. Simply say, "I will remember my dreams tonight." Keep a notebook by your bed and write down whatever you recall as soon as you wake. Over time, your ability to remember will strengthen.

Not every dream is literal. Many are symbolic, reflecting emotions or experiences that have not yet been processed. But even in their symbolism, they can offer guidance, insight, and healing. Many people have shared dream experiences that moved me deeply. One woman described a dream in which her late mother appeared and simply held her hand in silence. She woke up in tears—not tears of grief, but something she described as relief. She said, “I woke up knowing she was okay. I can’t explain how I knew. I just knew.”

Another client dreamed of her deceased husband sitting at their kitchen table, exactly as he used to, reading the newspaper. When she approached him, he looked up, smiled, and said, “You’re doing great.” She told me it was the most comforting thing she had experienced since his death. It did not make her feel sad. It made her feel accompanied.

If you are not currently experiencing dreams of your loved ones, please do not be discouraged. Readiness matters, and so does stress. If your nervous system is in a constant state of heightened alert, the deeper, quieter communication that happens during sleep may be harder to access. As you practice the principles in this book—creating stillness, developing intention, nurturing connection—you may find that the dreams come.

A Final Thought on Signs

Signs are not reserved for a select few. They are not limited to the deeply spiritual or the highly intuitive. They are available to all of us. They arrive through numbers, music, dreams, conversations, and moments that feel just a little too meaningful to ignore. The question is not whether signs exist. The question is whether you are willing to notice them. You likely have your own stories—moments you may have dismissed or kept to yourself out of fear of what others might think. I encourage you to revisit them. There may be more meaning there than you realized at the time. Your experiences are valid. Your story matters. And sometimes, the very thing you hesitate to share is exactly what someone else needs to hear.

Chapter 6: What Are Clairs?

"We each have a sixth sense that is attuned to the oneness dimension in life, providing a means for us to guide our lives in accord with our ideas."
~ Henry Reed

You may have heard of the clairs—a term used to describe a range of intuitive or psychic abilities that allow us to perceive beyond the ordinary limits of our five senses. These abilities expand how we experience the world, opening us to information that does not come through sight, sound, touch, taste, or smell alone.

There are six primary clairs: clairvoyance (clear seeing), clairaudience (clear hearing), clairsentience (clear feeling), claircognizance (clear knowing), clairsalience (clear smelling), and clairgustance (clear tasting). Each one represents a different way of receiving information from beyond the physical world as we typically understand it.

I believe that everyone possesses at least one of these abilities, whether they recognize it or not. The encouraging part is that they are not reserved for a gifted few—they can be developed. As your awareness deepens, these senses can become more refined, and through them, you may begin to feel a continued connection with your deceased loved ones.

For many, this becomes part of what I describe as moving into the seventh stage of grief—a stage not of separation, but of continued connection.

If you pause and reflect, you may already recognize moments in your life that point to these abilities. Have you ever felt something was about to happen before it did? Known something without being able to explain how? Followed a gut instinct that proved to be right? Found yourself in exactly the right place at the right time, as though guided there?

Many people dismiss these experiences as coincidence. I used to as well. But over time, I began to see them differently—not as random, but as meaningful. Whether you interpret them as intuition, heightened awareness, or something more spiritual, they are worth paying attention to.

As you begin to notice these moments, something subtle yet powerful begins to shift within you. Your awareness expands. You become more present, more attuned—not just to the external world, but to your internal one. Life begins to feel richer, more connected, and less accidental. You start to sense that there may be more happening beneath the surface than you once believed.

Why do these abilities exist? One way to understand them is as tools—ways of connecting to something beyond yourself. Some people describe this as God, others as Spirit, energy, or consciousness. However you define it, the experience is often similar: a sense of guidance, reassurance, or connection that feels real, even if it cannot be fully explained.

Not everyone experiences all six clairs. In fact, most people naturally resonate with one or two. Developing them does not require anything extraordinary. It begins with something simple: awareness. Awareness of your senses, your thoughts, your environment, and the subtle shifts that occur within you.

Start by paying attention to your everyday experiences. Are you noticing things you once overlooked? Feeling emotions more deeply? Picking up on the energy in a room? Hearing your inner voice more clearly? These are often the first signs that your awareness is expanding.

Clairvoyance: Clear Seeing

Clairvoyance, meaning "clear seeing," is the ability to receive information visually beyond ordinary sight. This may come in the form of mental images, symbols, flashes of insight, or even vivid dreams. It is often associated with the "mind's eye"—the ability to visualize something internally without physically seeing it.

People who are naturally visual—artists, designers, photographers—may find this ability comes more easily to them. But it is not limited to creative professions. Many people experience moments of seeing something in their mind before it happens or picturing something that later proves meaningful.

If you want to develop this ability, begin with stillness. Sit quietly, close your eyes, and allow your mind to settle. When you feel calm, invite an image to appear. Do not force it. Simply observe whatever comes. It may not make sense at first, and that is okay. Understanding often follows later.

The key is not to analyze immediately. The logical mind tends to interrupt the process. Instead, allow the image to exist without judgment. Over time, patterns may begin to emerge, and your trust in what you see will grow.

Clairaudience: Clear Hearing

Clairaudience is the ability to receive messages through sound—either as an internal voice or, more rarely, as something that feels external. This is not the same as ordinary thinking. It often feels distinct, as though the message arrives rather than being created. For some, this comes as a clear inner voice offering guidance or reassurance. For others, it may be hearing a song at the exact moment it is needed or sensing meaning in words spoken by someone else.

I experienced something like this after Steve died. There were moments when I would hear his name in my mind—not as a thought I was generating, but as something that arrived, unbidden and clear. At first, it startled me. Over time, I came to welcome it.

If you wish to develop clairaudience, begin by creating quiet. True quiet—not just the absence of external noise, but the quieting of your internal chatter. This is, admittedly, one of the most challenging practices in modern life. We are conditioned to fill every moment with stimulation. But in the silence, something often waits.

You might try sitting in stillness for five minutes each morning, simply listening. Not to anything in particular—just listening. Allow whatever arises to arise without chasing it or pushing it away. Over time, you may begin to notice a quality of inner listening that goes beyond what you expected.

Clairsentience: Clear Feeling

Clairsentience is perhaps the most commonly experienced of the clairs, though it is often the least recognized. It is the ability to feel the emotions or physical sensations of others—or to receive information through physical or emotional sensation.

If you have ever walked into a room and immediately felt the tension in it, before anyone said a word—that is clairsentience. If you have ever felt a sudden wave of emotion that seemed to belong to someone else, or felt the physical presence of a loved one who was not there—that, too, may be clairsentience.

Many people who are naturally empathic—who feel deeply, who are moved easily by the emotions of others—

have a strong clairsentient ability, though they may have spent years trying to manage it or tone it down. In a grief context, clairsentience can show up as a warm feeling in the room when you are thinking about your loved one, or a sudden sense of peace that seems to arrive from nowhere.

To develop clairsentience, practice tuning into your body. Before you enter a room or a conversation, notice what your body is already feeling. After an interaction, notice how your body feels differently. Begin to trust your physical responses as a form of information, not just sensation.

Claircognizance: Clear Knowing

Claircognizance is the ability to know something without knowing how you know it. It is a sudden, complete understanding that arrives without reasoning or evidence. It is the "I just know" experience.

This is how I knew I would one day live in Oak Park. It is how some people know, without being told, that something has happened to someone they love. It is how certain decisions feel immediately right, even when all logic argues against them. Many people have claircognizant experiences and dismiss them because they cannot be explained. But consider how often this kind of knowing has proved accurate in your own life. Consider the times you ignored it and wished you hadn't. Consider the times you trusted it and it led you exactly where you needed to go.

This ability often strengthens with age and life experience. The more loss you have moved through, the more practiced you become at accessing a form of wisdom that operates below the level of conscious thought. Grief, as painful as it is, can sharpen this sense in ways you may not yet recognize.

Clairsalience and Clairgustance: Clear Smelling and Tasting

The final two clairs—clairsalience (clear smelling) and clairgustance (clear tasting)—are less commonly discussed, but they are genuinely experienced and deserve acknowledgment.

Clairsalience is the ability to smell something that has no physical source. Many people who are grieving report suddenly smelling the perfume, aftershave, or cigarette smoke of a deceased loved one. These experiences are often brief and clear, and they frequently produce an immediate emotional response. I have experienced this with

Gerry. There are moments when I catch a scent that was distinctly his, in rooms where he has never been. These moments do not frighten me. They comfort me. They remind me that whatever form his energy has taken, it is not entirely absent from my life.

Clairgustance is the ability to taste something without any physical source. It is perhaps the rarest of the clairs, but those who experience it describe it as unmistakable—a sudden, specific taste that carries an immediate association.

Whether or not you experience these particular clairs, I want you to hold them as possibilities rather than impossibilities. Every sense we possess is a form of intelligence. And sometimes, intelligence arrives in ways that defy the ordinary.

Developing Your Intuitive Senses

The clairs are not a fixed gift you either have or you don't. They are capacities that can be cultivated, refined, and deepened over time. The most important thing you can do to develop them is not to seek dramatic experiences, but to practice presence.

Presence—the practice of being fully here, in this moment, with your senses open and your mind quiet—is the foundation of all intuitive awareness. Meditation, mindfulness, time in nature, and even the simple practice of walking slowly and noticing your surroundings can begin to open these channels.

Another important practice is trust. Many people experience intuitive moments and then immediately second-guess them. The mind steps in and offers an explanation, a reason to dismiss, a more "rational" interpretation. The practice of trusting your intuitive impressions—not blindly, but with gentle discernment—is what allows these senses to grow stronger.

Finally, create an environment that supports receptivity. This means reducing the constant noise of screens and busyness. It means carving out time for stillness, even briefly, each day. It means allowing yourself the luxury of doing nothing in particular—because it is often in those unscheduled moments that the most meaningful things arrive.

The clairs are not something you need to master before moving forward in this book. They are simply a lens—a way of naming what you may already be experiencing without yet having the words for it.

In Chapter 9, you will find real stories from real people that bring each of these abilities to life, not as theory but as lived experience. A hand appearing at a bedside. A name lighting up on a phone screen. A familiar scent drifting through a room where no physical source exists. A warm knowing that settles over someone at precisely the right moment. These are not exceptional people with rare gifts. They are ordinary grieving people who stayed open—and something came through. As you read their accounts, I invite you to look at them through the lens of the clairs. You may find that what once seemed mysterious suddenly has a name.

Reflection: *Which of the six clairs feels most familiar to you? Have you ever had an experience that might be described as intuitive or extrasensory? How did you respond to it at the time? What might it feel like to trust those experiences rather than dismiss them?*

Chapter 7: What Is the 7th Stage of Grief?

"Things we lose have a way of coming back to us in the end, if not always in the way we expect."
~ J.K. Rowling

You have arrived at the part of this book that everything else has been building toward. The 7th stage of grief is something I have not only lived, but named, embraced, and made central to both my life and my work. It builds upon the foundation laid by Elisabeth Kübler-Ross's five stages of grief and David Kessler's sixth stage, yet carries the journey one step further—into something deeper, more expansive, and ultimately more comforting than most people ever imagine. It is the stage where loss no longer feels like a complete ending, but instead becomes the beginning of a different kind of relationship.

The essence of the 7th stage is this: remaining open to receiving messages from your loved ones in the non-physical realm and allowing that connection to become a meaningful, integrated part of how you live your life. Every sign, every dream, every intuitive nudge, every moment of inexplicable knowing described in the previous chapters becomes part of this lived experience. It is not about wishful thinking or denial, but about awareness, openness, and a willingness to experience love in a new form.

When you pause and think about the person you have lost, you may realize that the connection never fully disappeared. There may have been moments—a song at the right time, a number that repeated, a dream that felt too real to dismiss—when you sensed something beyond coincidence. Perhaps you brushed those moments aside or explained them away. But what if they were not random? What if they were the beginning of something more—a continuation of a relationship that never truly ended, only changed form?

The Stages That Came Before

To understand the 7th stage fully, it is important to acknowledge what came before it. Elisabeth Kübler-Ross introduced the five stages of grief—denial, anger, bargaining, depression, and acceptance—through her work with terminally ill patients, offering a framework that later expanded to those experiencing loss. These stages, however, were never meant to be linear. Grief does not unfold in a straight line. You may feel acceptance one day and find yourself back in anger or sadness the next. You may experience several stages at once. Their purpose is not completion, but awareness—allowing you to process what arises so that you can continue moving forward.

David Kessler later introduced a sixth stage: meaning. He observed that after profound loss, some individuals begin to transform their pain into purpose. They ask deeper questions about life, love, and existence, allowing grief to shape them into someone more aware and intentional. His work resonated deeply with me, because I had already begun experiencing something beyond even that—something I would later come to define as the 7th stage.

After Steve died, I found myself living this stage without yet having the language for it. After Gerry died in 2019, the experience became clearer and more undeniable. The signs, the connection, the sense of ongoing communication—it was too consistent and meaningful to ignore. In 2021, I began sharing this concept publicly, and it has since become the foundation of my coaching work and the heart of this book.

Defining the 7th Stage

The 7th stage of grief is the realization that your bond with your loved one does not end when their physical life ends. Instead, it continues, evolves, and transforms into a new

kind of relationship—one that exists beyond the limitations of the physical world. This relationship is experienced through signs, dreams, intuitive feelings, and a deep inner knowing that they are still present in some form. Grief does not disappear, but it becomes integrated. You are not erasing your loss or pretending it did not happen; you are allowing it to become part of you in a way that no longer destroys you, but instead expands you. You begin to carry your loved one not as an absence, but as a presence.
This is what distinguishes the 7th stage from the others.

The earlier stages are experiences you move through, while the 7th stage becomes something you live. It is not something you complete, but something you embody. It is ongoing, evolving, and deeply personal. It does not require closure, because love itself does not require closure.

Not everyone reaches this stage, and it is important to acknowledge that. Some people remain in earlier stages, held there by guilt, anger, denial, or unresolved pain. If that is where you find yourself, there is nothing wrong with you. Grief is complex, and healing takes time. But if you have been willing to feel, to question, and to remain open, you are already moving toward something more.

How I Arrived Here

For me, arriving at the 7th stage was not quick or easy. It came through years of grief, therapy, journaling, dancing, and an unwavering commitment to healing. It came through moments when I wanted to shut down, but chose instead to stay open. It came through experiences I could not explain logically, but could feel deeply. It came through loss—deep, repeated loss—and through the decision, again and again, not to let those losses define the end of my story.

The 7th stage did not announce itself. It arrived gradually, through the accumulation of small moments that I chose to treat as meaningful rather than dismiss as coincidence. It arrived through the patterns I began to notice when I started paying attention. It arrived through the grief work I committed to, the support I sought, and the willingness to believe that love—real love—does not simply disappear because a body has.

I want to be clear about something: the 7th stage does not require you to stop grieving. It is not the end of grief. It is a new relationship with grief—one that makes room for both the loss and the love, simultaneously. In the 7th stage, grief and connection coexist. You can miss someone profoundly and still feel their presence. You can feel the absence of a person and, at the same moment, feel them near you. This paradox—the holding of both—is, I believe, one of the most profound capacities of the human heart.

Living the 7th Stage

Living in the 7th stage has taught me that love is not confined to the physical body. It transforms, and as it transforms, so do we. You can live a full, meaningful—even joyful—life without the physical presence of your loved one. That does not mean you stop missing them. It means you begin to experience them differently. They are still with you—in signs, in energy, in memory, and in the quiet moments when you feel them most.

Living beyond the earlier stages of grief means living with an open door between this world and the next. It means trusting what you feel, even when you cannot fully explain it. It means allowing love to continue, rather than believing it has ended. It also means giving yourself permission to be happy. This is one of the places where many grieving people get stuck. There can be a feeling—spoken or unspoken—that being happy somehow dishonors the person who died. That moving forward means leaving them behind. That joy is a betrayal.

I want to say this as clearly and as compassionately as I know how: that is not true. Your happiness is not a betrayal of the person you lost. In fact, in my experience, it is something they would most want for you. When I feel Gerry's presence most strongly, it is never in the form of sadness or reproach. It is in the form of encouragement. Pride. Love.

The 7th stage is not about pretending the loss did not happen. It is about discovering that loss, profound as it is, does not have to be the final word in your story. Love—real, enduring love—writes a different ending.

Reflection: *What if your relationship with your loved one has not ended at all? What if it has simply changed form and is waiting for you to notice? What would it mean for your daily life if you believed that to be true?*

Being open to that possibility may change everything. In the next chapter, I will share practical ways to help you begin—or deepen—your communication with those you have lost. Because the truth is, the conversation never truly ended. You simply needed to learn a new language.

Chapter 8: How to Live the 7th Stage of Grief

"They who are near me do not know that you are nearer to me than they are. You who are far away do not know that you are closer to me than those who are near."
~ Rabindranath Tagore

The idea of a continuing bond may feel unfamiliar at first. You may find yourself wondering how it is even possible to maintain a relationship with someone who is no longer physically present. The truth is, there are many ways—and none of them require special gifts or extraordinary abilities. They require only intention, attention, and a willingness to remain open. What follows are practices that have supported me and the many people I have guided through grief. I invite you to try them and notice what resonates.

Write to Them

Writing has long been a tool for healing. Research on expressive writing shows that when you write from your emotional core—not just recounting events, but truly feeling them—it can support both emotional and physical well-being. Writing to your loved one creates a bridge, a connection that allows thoughts and feelings to move freely. Over time, many people notice that when they reread what they have written, it feels as though the words came from somewhere beyond themselves. This is often referred to as automatic writing—the experience of allowing words to flow without conscious control. I experienced this myself in the letters I wrote to Steve after his death, especially one written on August 6, 2006. At the time, I did not understand what I was doing. I only knew I needed to do it.

If you feel called to try, find a quiet space. Take a few slow breaths and allow your mind to settle. Ask for guidance—whatever that means to you. Then begin to write. You may even try using your non-dominant hand to quiet the analytical mind. Do not force anything. Do not judge what comes. Let it unfold, and trust that meaning will reveal itself in time.

Speak to Them

Speaking to your loved ones is another powerful practice. I speak to Gerry about golf, to Steve about music, and to my sister Ralene about family. To some, this may seem unusual. To me, it feels completely natural. Sound is vibration. When you speak, you create waves that move through space, whether or not you can see where they land. We know that animals hear frequencies far beyond what humans can detect. After Steve died, I stayed at my daughter's home, and her dog, Payton, rarely left my side.

He seemed to understand my grief in a way that felt beyond words. It made me wonder if animals sense what we cannot.

I believe our loved ones exist as energy—pure vibration. Speaking to them is not a one-sided act. It is communication. And just as we trust that a pet hears us without speaking back, we can begin to trust that our loved ones are listening too. The question then becomes: are we listening?

Create Space for Silence

Listening begins with silence. Our world is filled with constant noise—external and internal. The mind alone produces tens of thousands of thoughts each day, most of them repetitive. In that noise, subtle awareness is easily lost. Creating moments of silence allows something deeper to emerge.

You can begin simply. Turn off the radio while driving. Walk outside and listen to the natural world—the wind, the birds, the rhythm of your own breath. Sit at home without distractions and notice what you hear when everything else is quiet. These are not just calming exercises. They are practices that train your awareness.

You may not hear a voice. You may instead feel a presence, a sense of calm, or a quiet knowing. That is enough. The goal is not to force an experience, but to create space for one.

Speak of Them to Others

As you move forward in life, speaking about your loved one becomes part of keeping that connection alive. They shaped who you are, and their presence—physical or not—continues to live through you. In new relationships, this requires balance. There is a time and place to share deeply. Communication matters. If someone struggles with your continuing bond, that is information worth paying attention to. You are not meant to hide your love or your grief, but to express it in ways that support connection rather than overwhelm it.

Live in a Way That Would Make Them Proud

Living in a way that would make your loved one proud can also become a powerful source of healing. Ask yourself what that means. Is there something you have been avoiding? A change you know you need to make? A dream you once shared? Often, grief reveals where growth is waiting.

I have seen this in my work with clients. One man, after losing his wife, found the strength to stop drinking—not for her, but for himself. Her presence became a source of support rather than pain. For me, it has shown up in simple ways, like improving my golf game after Gerry's death. When I play well, I feel his presence, his pride, his encouragement.

Keep Meaningful Belongings

Keeping meaningful belongings can also support connection. The goal is not to hold onto everything, but to honor what matters. Gerry's artwork fills my home. His belongings have been shared with family and friends, allowing his presence to extend outward in meaningful ways. These are not attachments—they are expressions of love.

Sometimes connection shows up in the smallest moments. Trying something your loved one enjoyed, even something as simple as I did—eating French fries the way Steve liked them. Those moments can bring you back to a shared memory. These are not acts of grief—they are moments of connection, small doorways between past and present.

Create Rituals

Creating rituals can deepen this connection. Lighting a candle, listening to music, or honoring a special date allows you to pause and remember intentionally. These rituals do not have to be elaborate. They simply need to be meaningful to you.

I often return to a line that has stayed with me: *it is better to remember and smile than to remember and remain in sorrow.* This is the essence of the 7th stage of grief—not forgetting but remembering differently.

These practices are not things you do once. They become part of how you live. They create a rhythm, a relationship, a way of moving through life with your loved ones still beside you.

Grief, Community, and the Healing Power of Belonging

One of the most important things I have learned in my years of grief work is that healing rarely happens in isolation. Human beings are wired for connection, and grief—which can be profoundly isolating—is one of the experiences that most urgently calls us back into community.

If you are not currently part of a grief support group or community, I encourage you to consider finding one. This does not have to be a formal clinical setting. It can be a small circle of people who have experienced loss and are willing to speak honestly about it. It can be an online community. It can be a grief retreat or workshop. What matters is the presence of others who understand, from the inside, what you are carrying.

There is something almost alchemical that happens when grieving people gather together with intention and openness. Stories are shared. Recognition occurs. The sense of being profoundly alone with your experience begins to dissolve. And in that dissolution, something opens—an access to your own grief that is sometimes difficult to find when you are navigating it alone.

I have witnessed this in workshops I have facilitated. People arrive cautiously, uncertain, often having kept their experiences to themselves for months or years. And then, as the stories begin to flow, something in the room shifts. People begin to recognize themselves in each other. The woman who thought she was imagining her husband's presence discovers that five other people in the room have had identical experiences. The man who felt he had to pretend he was fine discovers he doesn't have to pretend anymore. These moments of recognition are, I believe, some of the most healing available to us.

Grief and Joy: Giving Yourself Permission

As you develop the practices of the 7th stage, something unexpected may begin to happen, joy may start to return. Not the forced, performed happiness that the world sometimes asks of us, but genuine, quiet joy—moments of lightness, pleasure, even laughter.

When this happens, please do not push it away. Do not tell yourself you don't deserve it, or that it is too soon, or that feeling good is a betrayal of your grief. Joy and grief are not opposites. They are not in competition. They can and do exist side by side, in the same heart, sometimes in the same moment.

I remember the first time I laughed—genuinely laughed—after Steve died. It was something small and silly, something my daughter said. And the laughter felt strange in my body, like a muscle that had not been used in a long time. And then it felt like relief. And then it felt like guilt. That cycle—relief, then guilt—is something many grieving people experience when joy begins to return. It is normal. And it is something that, with time and intention, you can move through.

You are allowed to feel good. You are allowed to have moments of happiness. You are allowed to find that life still holds beauty, even alongside profound loss. This is not a betrayal of the person you lost. It is, I believe, exactly what they would want for you. It is, in fact, one of the ways their love continues to work in your life—through the joy they have made possible, simply by having been part of it.

Navigating Anniversaries, Birthdays, and Holidays

One of the practical challenges of living in grief is navigating the recurring calendar—anniversaries, birthdays, holidays, and other dates that hold particular significance. These can be times of ambush, when grief that has softened suddenly sharpens again. They can feel like a test, as though you should have made more progress by now, should be able to get through the day without falling apart.

I want to offer a different frame. These recurring dates are not tests. They are invitations. They are the moments the calendar carves out for you to pause, to remember, to feel, and to connect. Rather than dreading them, consider meeting them with intention.

Create a plan for how you want to honor the day. This might mean lighting a candle and listening to their favorite music. It might mean gathering with people who loved them and sharing stories. It might mean doing something the two of you used to do together, or something you know they would have loved. It might mean sitting quietly with a photograph and allowing yourself to feel whatever arises, without judgment or interruption.

What I have found, over years of navigating these dates, is that the anticipation of them is often harder than the day itself. When you approach a significant date with dread, the dread builds in the days leading up to it and can be more debilitating than the date itself. When you approach it with intention—with a plan for how you will honor it—the day often holds both grief and something else: love, memory, connection, even gratitude.

If the holidays are particularly challenging—as they often are—give yourself permission to restructure them. You do not have to celebrate in exactly the way you always did. You do not have to attend every gathering, or host the dinner, or maintain every tradition unchanged. Grief is not a temporary inconvenience that will be resolved by the next holiday season. It is part of your life now, and your life, including your holidays, can be restructured to honor it.

Some people find it helpful to create a new tradition alongside the old ones—one that explicitly honors the person who is missing. An empty chair at the table. A donation in their name. A moment of shared remembrance before the meal. These gestures do not require long explanations to the people around you. They simply require your willingness to claim the space that love deserves.

Grief as a Spiritual Practice

I want to close this chapter by naming something that I believe is true, even if it sounds counterintuitive: grief, fully met, is a spiritual practice.

By spiritual, I do not mean religious, though for some people religious practice is where they find the most support. By spiritual, I mean the practice of attending to what is most essentially real—love, connection, meaning, impermanence, and the mystery of consciousness itself.

When you sit with grief rather than running from it, you are practicing presence. When you allow yourself to feel the full depth of loss, you are practicing honesty. When you continue to love someone who is no longer physically here, you are practicing a form of love that transcends the ordinary conditions we put on it. These are not trivial acts. They are profound ones.

Grief strips away the superficial. It confronts you with what matters. It removes the illusion that you are in control, that life will proceed as planned, that the people you love will always be present. And in the stripping away, something is revealed: the bare, essential fact of love, and the bare, essential fact that love does not need a body to exist.

The 7th stage of grief is, at its heart, a spiritual stance toward loss. It is the stance of someone who has looked directly at the hardest thing and chosen, nonetheless, to remain open. To remain connected. To remain in love, even with someone who can no longer be touched.

That stance is one of the most courageous and most beautiful things a human being can practice. And it is available to you, exactly where you are.

Chapter 9: Signs, Synchronicity, and Daily Connection

"Those we love don't go away, they walk beside us every day…unseen, unheard, but always near, still loved, still missed, and very dear." ~ author unknown

Everything in this book has been moving toward this chapter. The grief defined, the death examined, the pain named, the stages mapped, the clairs explored, the practices offered—all of it has been preparation. This chapter is where the living proof arrives. It is the place where the 7th stage stops being a concept and becomes something you can hold in your hands.

What follows are stories. Mine, and the stories of others who were willing to share what they have witnessed. I offer them not as proof of anything—proof is not the point—but as companionship. As evidence that you are not imagining things. As a reminder that the language of a continuing bond is spoken quietly, all around you, by people who may look perfectly ordinary from the outside but who are carrying something extraordinary inside. These are people who are living in the 7th stage of grief, whether or not they have ever called it that. They are paying attention. They are staying open. And what they are experiencing is real.

Pay Attention to the Unexpected

The deceased communicate in ways we do not always anticipate. One night I woke around 12:15 a.m. with an excruciating headache. I went to the living room and opened YouTube on my television, intending to find a meditation. Instead, a doctor appeared on my screen—a specialist in sinus and headache relief—demonstrating exactly the massage technique I needed. I had never searched for anything like it. I had never watched anything remotely similar. Yet there he was, plain as day, in my living room at midnight.

I sat with him for thirty minutes and went back to bed with relief. I knew it was Gerry. Of course it was a doctor. Gerry knew I would only trust a medical professional—and so he sent one. I thanked him before I fell back asleep.

The next morning, I opened my refrigerator and a glass dish shattered on the floor. Broken glass carries many meanings. In Jewish tradition, a groom breaks a glass at his wedding—as Gerry did at ours—to symbolize the fragility of relationships and the beginning of a new life together.

Spiritually, broken glass can represent transformation, the courage to move forward, and the reminder not to dwell on what has been lost. I heard Gerry's message clearly: *Let go of the life we had in the physical. Allow new people and experiences in. I am always with you. Go live your life and love again.*

It was exactly what I needed to hear. And it did not surprise me that he chose glass—he was, after all, a glass-blowing artist. He always had a flair for the meaningful gesture.

Numbers, Dragonflies, and the Forms Spirit Takes

I have described at length the role of numbers in my life—the 1's and 11's that have guided me since 2006, the patterns that continue to appear daily on clocks, receipts, addresses, and flight seats. After Gerry died, new numbers arrived: 555, 333, and 222, each carrying their own resonance and meaning.

Carl Jung defined synchronicity as a meaningful coincidence of two or more events where something other than chance is involved. When you encounter a number, a song, an animal, or an object at precisely the moment you need it, that is synchronicity at work. It originates from beyond the conscious mind, and it is one of the primary languages through which the spirit realm communicates.

Numerology—the study of the vibratory power of numbers—has roots stretching back to the ancient world. Pythagoras, considered the father of modern numerology, believed that numbers hold the key to personality, desire, and life path. Both Steve and Gerry share the life path number 1—a fact I did not discover until after they were gone. I do not believe it is a coincidence.

After Gerry died, a dragonfly came to rest beneath my patio chair and stayed there, motionless, for fifteen minutes—entirely undisturbed by my presence. The following day it returned and then was gone. The next day it returned, but I found it lifeless and gently placed it in a bowl, where it remains, resembling a small piece of glass art. Which is fitting, because Gerry crafted exquisite glass pieces in his studio. Each time I see the dragonfly, I feel his energy—translated, as energy always is, into a form I would recognize.

Can the spirit of the deceased enter an animal, a number, a song, a broken dish? I cannot prove it. But I remain open to all possibilities—and the more open I have become, the more I have witnessed. The signs are there for everyone. Most people simply have not been taught to look.

A Grasshopper and a Beach Full of Glass

On September 7, 2020, a tiny grasshopper landed unexpectedly on my kitchen windowsill in Michiana. As I watched it, a sense of warmth and safety moved through me. I researched its symbolism and found that grasshoppers can only move forward—they are physically incapable of moving backward. What a metaphor for grief. They produce sound vibrations believed to foster a deep connection to the earth and the soul, and their presence is considered a powerful omen of abundance and spiritual prosperity. I knew immediately it was a message from Gerry and it was one I needed that day.

In the months that followed, new numbers began appearing in my daily life. Where I had previously been guided by 11:11 and 1:11, I now began seeing 555, 333, and 444 almost daily. On April 6, 2020—a date that reduces to a "1" vibration in numerology—I saw 11:11, 3:33, 4:44, and 5:55 on the clock throughout that single day. I stopped counting coincidences a long time ago. These are not coincidences.

On September 14, 2023, the eighteenth anniversary of Steve's death, I shared the following post on my Suicide Survivors Facebook page. I share it here because grief shared openly can help others feel less alone—and because Steve deserves to be remembered:

On 9/14/23, 18 years ago, my beloved husband Steve died by suicide. It's been a difficult journey, but I am a survivor and have been transformed by all that has happened. In those years, I watched my granddaughter grow, and we celebrated her 18th birthday on 9/11. Sadly, she never knew Steve, but he held her in his arms the day she was born. Three days later, he died. In that tragedy, I was grateful for her life. She has been a source of joy for all our family.

In 2011, I felt blessed to marry again, and sadly, Gerry suddenly died in our home in 2019. Despite the tragedies, I would not trade the pain for the love I have shared with those amazing men.

Steve played the guitar and loved playing the Beatles' music, so I honor him today by lighting a candle and listening to the Beatles. The morning of 9/14/23, I lit the candle and asked Alexa to play Beatles music, and she played 'Blackbird'—one of Steve's favorites. I then looked at my email and found my daily trivia quiz: 'The Beatles record label was named after which fruit?' The quiz was entirely about the Beatles. It was not ironic. It was Steve's way of connecting with me.

Later, I walked on the beach and found ten pieces of beach glass. Steve's life path number is 1. Ten pieces of glass is the energy of 1. I also found a rock in the shape of a heart. Steve was sending me the message that love lives on. That evening, I reached into my joy jar and pulled out a note that read: 'You are a survivor.' These are not coincidences. These are signs. It is a matter of paying attention to them.

I am certain you have signs of your own. Pay attention to them. Treasure them. They are meant for you.

My Brother Russel

In March 2024, while working on this book, I mentioned to my brother Russel—a research scientist—that I was writing about dreams and connecting with the deceased. I was not sure how he would respond. Science guides his thinking, and I had never heard him speak about experiences like mine. But he surprised me. He told me that he had struggled deeply with the death of our grandmother, who passed away in 2007 at the age of 92.

One night, during his grief, he had a dream. Our grandmother came to him and told him not to be sad for her—that everything was good, and that everything would be alright for him. He woke to find her standing at the foot of his bed. He did not believe it was a dream. He believed she was there.

I explained that what he experienced is called *a visit*—that the departed have the power to return in a form that human souls can perceive. Russel told me he believed it. That surprised me, given how firmly his worldview is rooted in science. But as I have said throughout this book: experiencing these things for yourself makes you a believer. My brother became one.

I share Russel's story here for a reason. If a research scientist—someone whose entire professional life is built on empirical evidence and the rigorous testing of claims—can be moved to belief by a single experience in the night, then perhaps the question is not whether these experiences are real, but whether we are willing to remain open enough to receive them. My brother was open, in his grief. And something came through.

Stories from Others Who Are Living Beyond Loss

The experiences I have shared in this chapter are my own—but they are not unusual. All around us, people are quietly living in connection with those they have lost, often without a framework for what they are experiencing. The following stories were shared with me by people willing to give voice to what they have witnessed. I offer them as gifts—not as proof, but as belonging. As a reminder that you are part of a much larger community of people who are learning, as you are, to speak the language of continuing love.

The Touch — by Gina Donaldson, Lisle, Illinois

My beloved husband Dru died by suicide in 2005. I was devastated and lived in grief for many years, made heavier still by the loss of more loved ones in the years that followed.

In 2008, my mother was diagnosed with stage three lung cancer. She was my biggest cheerleader, and we were extraordinarily close. We talked every day, and I stayed with her most days and nights as her health declined. My heart broke in January 2010 when she died. I was not sure I could go on without her.

Shortly after she died, I visited a Reiki practitioner at the Wellness House, a nonprofit center offering mental, physical, and spiritual resources for cancer patients and their families. During my session, as I lay on the table, I felt the practitioner's hands moving through my energy field. My eyes were closed, and I was deeply peaceful. I sensed the practitioner was standing at my feet. Then I felt two hands at my feet—and another hand at my shoulder. My mind registered the impossibility quietly: she cannot have three hands.

I did not want to break the peace, but I could not resist. I opened my eyes. There, next to my hand, was a wrinkled hand. Not the practitioner's—she was young. I knew immediately whose it was. It was my mother's hand.
I heard her voice in my mind tell me I was at peace, and that all would be well. It made me a believer that we can maintain a real connection with our loved ones after they die. Thank you, Mom. I love you.

My Favorite Angel — by Gloria Moro, Long Branch, New Jersey

Several years ago, my sister-in-law Margaret was battling leukemia. We had known each other for more than fifty years and shared a rich life together—visits to communes in the seventies when she lived a hippie lifestyle, celebrations when she earned her BA, MS, and PhD, weekend retreats, six weeks in Italy, and a mutual spiritual journey that deepened us both.

I spend my winters in Florida, and when Margaret died, I was not in New Jersey to be with her at the end. I told my daughter I wished I had asked Margaret for a sign. Several days later, my "Favorites" screen appeared on my iphone with only one name on it: MARGARET. I had not known that screen existed. I had never written her name on it. I have no explanation for how it appeared.

Over the years since, whenever that screen pops up, I smile and feel a warm current move through my body. In the weeks before I wrote this story, she appeared several times. I believe she was urging me to get it written so she could be in this book. Typical Margaret—always finding a way to make herself known.

A Tribute to Sue's Love — by Bev Hierl, Ohio

Those of us who have lost someone we deeply love desperately hope that they are still aware of us—still looking out for us. I believe they are, because of what happened between my brother-in-law Tom and me after his wife Sue died.

Sue and Tom had been married for sixty years when she died of ovarian cancer in 2016. They were role models to everyone who knew them—for the way they loved each other and raised their seven children. I had been close to Sue over the years, though Tom and I barely knew each other beyond brief family holidays.

When our family received the news of Sue's death, I made the ten-hour trip to attend the funeral with my children. The funeral home was overflowing. When I finally reached Tom in the receiving line, he looked confused for a moment—and then hugged me for a long time, like a long-lost friend. I didn't know how to respond. He didn't know me well. I expressed my condolences and moved on, but I was struck by how desolate he appeared. Driving home, I told my children I wouldn't be surprised if we had to make the same trip the following year.

For months afterward, I thought of Tom often. At Christmas, I wrote him a brief note on a card, telling him I was thinking of him and sending peace to his family. A week later, I received a lengthy letter in return. He told me that Sue had been making her presence felt at his shoulder regularly—urging him to contact me. He had felt hesitant, unsure of my response. He asked if I would be willing to correspond, because he needed someone to connect with and didn't want to burden his grieving children further.

I wrote back. I shared my own experience of feeling my father's peaceful presence after his death, hoping it would reassure Tom that he was not imagining things. And in his next letter, he told me something that stopped me entirely.

When he first saw me standing in the waiting line at the funeral home, a warm, peaceful feeling had washed over him—and he had known, without understanding why, that everything was going to be alright. That same feeling returned whenever he thought of me. Sue would then connect with him and remind him to reach out.

We spent months getting to know each other through letters and emails. Tom eventually told me he believed it was our destiny to be together. I had feelings for him too, but I had been in a difficult marriage and had vowed never to let myself become vulnerable again. Still, I needed to know whether Sue's presence was real or grief-induced imagination. So, I spoke to her directly. I asked her to send me a sign if she was truly trying to bring us together.

Two days later, my sister Kathryn was visiting. We were at my computer preparing to order concert tickets when she said, "Bev, I have to share a special email I just received—I thought of you when I read it." She found it and handed it to me. It was an article recently published in the New York Times, written by a woman dying of ovarian cancer—just as Sue had died. The article was titled "You Might Want to Marry My Husband." The woman described her husband as a wonderful father and partner, and she was looking for someone special to love and care for him after she was gone.

I read it and said aloud: "That's it. That's the sign." Tom and I spent a weekend together the following month. From that point on, we were never apart, and we married in 2018. We had seven wonderful years together before Tom passed away in May 2024. I am profoundly grateful for every one of those years—for the precious gift of true love he gave me, just as he had once given it to Sue. And I am certain they are both smiling as I write this.

A Jar of Love — by Ellyn Vogel, Indiana

My mother was a strong woman—a presence that filled every room she entered. As a music teacher, she conducted a children's choir, and her voice was warm, commanding, and full of life. It could lift the spirits of an entire classroom or quiet it with a single gentle *shush.* Even in stillness, you could feel her strength in the cadence of her speech, the warmth in her laughter, and the joy she carried in every melody she shared.

Then came the diagnosis: tongue cancer. The woman whose voice had once filled hearts and classrooms now faced unimaginable suffering. Most of her tongue had to be removed, leaving her unable to speak or eat. Her powerful voice was silenced, and her body weakened—yet the strength in her eyes never wavered. Watching her suffer was excruciating, especially while caring for my own two small children, who needed me even as I longed to hold my mother close.

During chemotherapy and radiation, almost everything became unbearable for her. She complained that everything smelled bad. Then my cousin brought her a special cream for her dry, burned skin. The moment my mother applied it, she smiled—a fleeting, precious smile—and said it was the only thing that felt good and smelled good to her. That cream became a rare thread of comfort amid her suffering.

After she passed, grief consumed me. I longed for any sign that she was no longer in pain and was at peace. Months later, living in a different state, I walked into my bathroom—and there on the countertop was the jar of cream that had been by her bed. I had no idea how it had come to be there. I blinked, certain I was imagining things. Then I reached for it with trembling hands, opened the lid, and the familiar scent washed over me—along with her presence, her touch, and her love. Her fingerprints were still in the cream.

For a moment it felt as though she were reaching through the jar to touch my face and my heart. From that day on, whenever I want to feel close to her, I open the jar. I see her prints. I smell her. And I am reminded that her love endures, even beyond death.

Her struggle was immense, and my grief runs deep. But the jar of cream reminds me that love never truly leaves us.

Even when someone we cherish is gone, their presence can find a way to touch our hearts, to reassure us, and to guide us back toward hope. Look closely—you may find your own version of the jar. A scent, an object, a song, a screen that lights up with a name you did not put there. The signs are waiting. All you have to do is pay attention.

Build a Morning Practice

Living in the 7th stage of grief eventually becomes as natural as any daily habit. The invitation is to weave your connection to your deceased loved ones into your daily routine—intentionally, lovingly, and consistently.

After Gerry died, I established a morning practice that has anchored me ever since. I begin by saying good morning to the universe and to Gerry. I ask Alexa to play "It's a Beautiful Morning" by the Rascals—a song Steve loved— and let its opening notes set the tone for the day. Over coffee, I read something inspirational. Then I ring my Tibetan singing bowls and let their vibrations settle into me before the day begins. I exercise outdoors when I can—nature is essential to healing, and movement keeps the body and the spirit in conversation.

This is my practice. Yours will look different. The point is to have one—a daily, intentional act of connection that says: I am still here. So are you. Let us move through this day together.

Have you created a morning practice for yourself? If not, now is the time. Start small. Say good morning to your loved one. Make the coffee. Play the song. Light the candle. Begin.

Some people resist the idea of a morning practice because they fear it will intensify their grief. My experience, and the experience of many people I have worked with, is the opposite. A brief, intentional moment of connection at the start of the day does not open a floodgate of pain. It creates a container for grief that is manageable, even beautiful. It transforms grief from something that ambushes you unpredictably into something you actively hold with care and intention. That shift—from ambushed to intentional—is one of the most significant changes I have seen in people moving into the 7th stage.

When No Signs Come

There are days when I feel nothing. No songs arrive unexpectedly. No dreams carry a message. In those moments, my faith does not waver—because I have learned that the absence of a sign is not the absence of presence. As sure as the sun rises, I trust that connection will return. And it always does.

You may live alone now. But you are not alone. Your higher power, your angels, and your loved ones are near—in the stillness, in the synchronicities, in the small moments you might otherwise walk past without noticing. The writer Mitch Albom understood this when he wrote that the only time we waste is the time we spend thinking we are alone. Living in the 7th stage of grief is living in the awareness that you never truly are.

The following poem has brought comfort to grieving people around the world for nearly a century. As you read it, allow yourself to think of your loved one. Notice where you feel them. Notice what arises.

Do not stand at my grave and weep, I am not there; I do not sleep. I am a thousand winds that blow, I am the diamond glints on snow, I am the sunlight on ripened grain, I am the gentle autumn rain. When you awaken in the morning's hush I am the swift uplifting rush Of quiet birds in circled flight. I am the soft stars that shine at night. Do

not stand at my grave and cry; I am not there. I did not die.
~ Mary Frye

I have felt Gerry in the morning light. I have felt Steve in the music that finds me when I least expect it. I have felt Ralene in the quiet moments when I needed my sister most. They are not gone. They are everywhere—if you know how to look.

A New Language

I saw a post recently that said: *I don't think I will ever get used to saying "was" after your name.* My response is simple—you don't have to. Say "is." Keep them in the present tense if that brings you comfort. When I sense Gerry nearby, I say: Gerry is here. He is watching. He is pleased. Language is yours to shape. You have the freedom to speak of your loved ones however feels most true.

The 7th stage of grief does not ask you to stop grieving. It asks you to let grief become something larger than loss—a living relationship, a continuing bond, a way of moving through the world with your loved ones still beside you. It is, I believe, one of the most beautiful ways a human being can choose to live.

You have now read this entire book. You have walked through grief defined and death examined. You have explored pain and suffering, signs and clairs, the science of the brain and the mystery of the spirit. You have read stories of hands appearing at bedsides, names lighting up on phone screens, grasshoppers that cannot move backward, jars of cream carrying fingerprints that outlasted a life. You have arrived here—at the place where all that knowledge becomes a practice, and all that pain becomes a doorway.

My wish for you is this: that you walk through it. That you speak their names. That you light the candle. That you eat the French fry with ketchup. That you dance—even when it is hard, especially when it is hard—and that in the dancing, you feel them beside you.

With love and light,

Robin

Epilogue

You have reached the end of this book, but not the end of your journey. Everything you have read—the science, the stories, the signs, the stages—has been pointing toward a single truth: that love does not end at death, and neither does your relationship with those you have lost. What changes is the language. This epilogue is an invitation to keep learning that language, and to know that others, all around you, are learning it too.

A Note on Thanatology

Thanatology is the scientific study of death and dying, and it is a field worth knowing exists. Thanatologists are specialists who focus on the dying process or work directly with those facing death, either their own or a loved one's.

The field includes a wide variety of practitioners: doctors, nurses, psychologists, cultural historians, music thanatologists who bring sound to the bedside of the dying, pastoral counselors, medical ethicists, and death doulas—non-medical professionals who emerged around the year 2000 to provide emotional and spiritual support to the dying and their families.

If any of these paths resonates with you, I encourage you to explore further. Knowledge of death, as I hope this book has shown, is ultimately knowledge of life.

A Closing Story

One of the most moving stories I have encountered in my work came from Diane Scribner, a Unity Minister, who shared the experience of a woman nearing the end of her life. As the woman took her final breaths, her daughter asked, "Mom, how do you feel?" The mother replied, "I am so excited to go to my new home."

I have thought about that response many times. Not everyone arrives at death's door with that kind of peace and anticipation—but the fact that some do tells us something profound. That woman was not afraid. She was not resisting. She was ready—and she was looking forward.

I do not know with certainty what awaits any of us. But I have come to believe, through everything I have lived and witnessed and been told, that what waits is not nothing. That love does not simply stop. That the people we have carried in our hearts continue, in some form, to carry us in theirs.

That belief has sustained me through losses that could have destroyed me. It has given me a framework for my grief and a reason to remain open when everything in me wanted to shut down. It has brought me to this book, and to you. Keep going. Keep talking to them. Keep watching for the signs. Keep lighting the candle. Keep saying their names in the present tense. They are listening. I am certain of it.

Continue the Journey

If this book touched you, please consider leaving a short review on Amazon. Your words help other readers find comfort and support.

You may also find comfort and insight in Robin's Grief and Healing Collection. Each book explores a different perspective on navigating loss and finding meaning again.

Be Gentle with Me, I'm Grieving — An award-winning book offering compassionate reflections from Robin's personal journey after the suicide of her husband.

Moving to Excellence: A Pathway to Transformation After Grief — A thoughtful exploration of how grief can eventually lead to growth, strength, and renewed purpose.

3 Must Have Connections for Inner Peace — A gentle guide to the essential connections that help restore balance, deepen spiritual awareness, and rediscover peace within.

Ten Grief Lessons from Golf — A unique and reflective book that reveals what the game of golf can teach us about patience, resilience, and healing after loss.

About the Author

Robin Chodak is grief coach and an author, who writes to support those navigating loss and searching for meaning after life's most difficult experiences. Her journey into grief work began after the suicide of her second husband in 2005. What began as personal journaling—letters written each night to stay connected and process her emotions became the foundation for a deeper sense of purpose. Through her own healing, Robin discovered a passion for helping others find hope and direction after loss.

Robin is a certified grief, life, and spiritual coach, as well as a certified Master NLP (Neuro-Linguistic Programming) practitioner and Reiki practitioner. She offers one-on-one coaching and has created an online course for those who desire to become a grief coach.

Her writing has appeared in publications including The Daily Word, the American Foundation for Suicide Prevention, Catholic Charities Loving Outreach to Suicide Survivors, and SOSBSA—Survivors of Suicide Bereavement Support Australia. She has also contributed to the anthologies *Tales of Our Lives: Fork in the Road* and

From Grief to Greatness. She was also featured in the *Chicago District Golf Digest.*

After finding love again and marrying Dr. Gerald Chodak, Robin experienced another profound loss when he died unexpectedly in their home in 2019. This season of grief deepened her understanding of the grieving process and further inspired her writing and her work supporting others.

Robin divides her time between Florida and Michiana. She continues to write, speak, and offer encouragement to those finding their way forward after loss.

Work With Robin

If this book resonated with you and you are navigating grief in your own life, Robin offers additional ways to support your healing journey.

One-on-One Grief Coaching — Personal coaching for individuals seeking guidance, understanding, and support during grief and life transitions.

Grief Coach Certification Online Program — For those who feel called to help others through loss, Robin has created an online program designed to train and certify compassionate grief coaches.

Additional Resources: Udemy courses —
Be Gentle with Me, I'm Grieving
Grief, A New Way of Thinking
Change Your Brain, Create an Excellent Life

To learn more or connect with Robin, visit

www.robinchodak.com

www.ingramcontent.com/pod-product-compliance
Lightning Source LLC
LaVergne TN
LVHW010929110826
845149LV00013B/2524

9780998708850